Praise for
Bruised Not Broken

Kristine Jensen's book is for anyone who wants to understand and overcome lifelong patterns of living in states of chronic shame. Grounding her work in a synchrony of theory and sharing everyday stories to illustrate her points, Jensen writes clearly and directly to those who struggle, offering much useful advice as well as kind company on their journey of healing.

> —**Patricia DeYoung, MSW, PhD**, author of *Understanding and Treating Chronic Shame: Healing Right Brain Relational Trauma* and *Shame and Grace: Six Essays on Falling Apart and Becoming Whole Again*

Kristine Jensen dives deep into the subject of shame, addressing such issues as why shame is at the root of depression, anxiety, and feelings of unworthiness and how shame is passed down from generation to generation through widely used parenting practices. *Bruised Not Broken* is filled with case examples and touching stories of her clients' and Jensen's own struggles with shame. This healing book uses a wide-ranging variety of strategies, including self-compassion, self-soothing, and self-forgiveness, to help anyone who suffers from deep shame, especially survivors of child abuse and neglect. I recommend this book to anyone who suffers from debilitating shame.

> —**Beverly Engel, LMFT,** author of *Escaping Emotional Abuse: Healing the Shame You Don't Deserve* and *Freedom at Last: Healing the Shame of Childhood Sexual Abuse*

This book is a must-read for anyone interested in understanding how shame affects their emotional and social well-being. Relevant to a broad audience, including individuals, therapists, clients, and anyone engaged in exploring how shame manifests internally and influences their lives, *Bruised Not Broken* is skillfully written and offers comprehensive insights into the various facets of this debilitating syndrome. Each chapter includes helpful summaries, reflection questions, and practical activities, enhancing its value as a tool for personal growth and understanding.

> —**Phyllis Watts, PhD**. Consulting and Clinical Psychologist

Kristine Jensen offers profound insights into understanding and overcoming our critical inner voices and healing the early childhood wounds that gave rise to them. In remarkably open and candid ways, she provides us with specific, actionable steps we can take for our own healing. Her guidance inspires hope and motivates us to embark on a transformative healing journey. This is a long overdue book that therapists, clients, and any of us who have experienced such feelings of unworthiness, will return to again and again.

—**Jacqueline Horn, PhD**. Emerita Faculty, University California, Davis

BRUISED NOT BROKEN

Healing the Shame
of a Troubled Childhood

*If one could grant a wish to improve
the well-being of humanity,
it would be to do away with shame.
The collective sigh of relief would be heard in distant galaxies.*
—The School of Life

Kristine B. Jensen, LCSW

ISBN: 979-8-9905950-2-6 (softcover)
ISBN: 979-8-9905950-1-9 (ebook)

Published by On Purpose Publishing
bruisednotbrokenbook.com
kristine-jensen.com

Interior design by Jill Ronsley, suneditwrite.com

Printed and bound in the USA

This book is intended to provide insights and guidance, and while the content draws on therapeutic principles and practices, it is not a substitute for professional mental health care. Each person's healing process is unique, and readers are encouraged to approach this resource with self-awareness and to prioritize their mental well-being by seeking appropriate professional help when necessary.

In this book, names and circumstances are altered to protect the privacy and confidentiality of individuals whose stories and experiences are shared. Any resemblance to actual persons, living or deceased, or actual events is coincidental. The alterations are made with the utmost respect for the privacy of those involved. This precautionary measure is taken to uphold ethical standards and prioritize the well-being and privacy of those whose stories contribute to the narrative.

My deepest thanks to the clients who shared their remarkable healing journeys. You have inspired me with your resilience and courage by showing me the power of the human spirit to heal and be whole despite whatever might have happened in the past. Thank you for your trust. I could not have authored this book without you.

Contents

Preface

Why read this book?

No one gets through childhood unscathed. Read this book
if you:

- are plagued by frequent thoughts that you are not
  good enough, unworthy, or broken.
- have emotional storms and sometimes feel out of
  control.
- are suspicious of the good and expect the worst.
- felt misunderstood by a parent or caretaker who
  attributed motives, feelings, and thoughts to you
  that were not true.
- fear getting close to people, worrying they will see
  how broken you are.
- keep parts of yourself hidden and feel like a fraud.
- feel ashamed of feeling ashamed.
- are tired of feeling so miserable and want to
  understand and heal your suffering.
- would like to know what shame is to understand or
  help someone you know.

This book offers a unique way of looking at the wounds of
a troubled childhood and their relationship to shame. Unique

because it traces the origins to preverbal experiences. Why is this important? Because to heal those wounds, it is essential to understand where it started, what caused it and how it shows up in adults. Depression, anxiety, poor self-esteem, self-contempt, and other mental health issues like narcissistic personality disorder and borderline personality disorder share a common core: shame.

A perspective about childhood shame

The origins of shame, whether from the thoughtless neglect of a self-absorbed mother, a blatantly abusive father, an absent or intoxicated caregiver, all have one thing in common: the child experiences an invalidation of their feelings and are ignored, scolded, or punished, for their natural needs for comfort, love, and a sense of safely belonging to someone who treasures them.

But my childhood wasn't that bad

You may not think of your childhood as unhappy or traumatic. You may have no memories of abuse; you were fed, clothed, and sent to school. But what is traumatic to a child is not just what happened to them. It can also be what was missing.

You may also have no memories of being comforted or hardly remember being played with. You may have been raised by siblings, childcare workers who came and went, or a harried, overwhelmed mother. Reliable, consistent emotional connection and emotional nurturing were missing.

This is traumatic for a baby or child. Whether it is trauma with a little t or trauma with a big T, when there is repeated emotional invalidation or emotional neglect, it is harmful to a child's development of the sense of self—self-esteem, self-confidence, and self-resilience. This kind of trauma is the breeding ground for shame.

My childhood was miserable

Wounds of abuse can be healed. Shame can be healed. Despite what you may have feared, you don't need to have a lifetime of suffering. Based on the current trauma treatment research, the experiences of many women and men I have worked with throughout my career as a psychotherapist, and my personal journey healing my own shame, the following pages outline a practical path you too can take. It is not an easy path, but it is a possible path. I provide exercises and straightforward steps that, if you pursue them with focus and intention, adding other aids that work for you, can enable you to heal your wounds and change the false beliefs you have about yourself and others. As you use the strategies I discuss, you can gain the power to meet this destructive venom called shame and gradually spit it out of your life.

Read on, do the work, be determined, never give up, and be one who knows what life feels like beyond the shame of a troubled childhood.

PART 1

UNDERSTANDING SHAME

Introduction

Shame is about our very selves. We feel unacceptable. It is not as if a few seams in the garment of our selves needs stitching, the whole fabric is frayed. And to feel that is a life-weary heaviness.

—Lewis Smedes

Almost before she sat down, my client blurted, "What is wrong with me? Why do I feel like I'm not good enough so much of the time?"

"I think I was born with it. Even as a little girl, I remember feeling something was wrong with me. You know—I didn't fit in, I was kind of weird, not like the other girls. I thought I would outgrow it, but here I am at fifty-five." She paused. "And in the rare moments I do feel okay, like at work, I immediately think I'm just faking it, and someone will find out. I'm sick of it. What the hell is wrong with me? I feel like something is broken in me and I don't think I'll ever feel good enough." Sandy looked away.

Sandy was not a newcomer to personal growth, and we had worked together for several months. We had explored her relationship with her mother in detail, we had searched her growing up years and early college looking for contributors to what I had labeled as poor self-esteem. But her life was filled with memories of birthday parties, friends, off to college, and then finding fulfilling work in a non-profit that she loved. Later she married a man she described as loving but quiet.

But what I failed to appreciate was how significant her history was as an infant. Sandy was placed with an aunt who had her own two young children and a six-month-old for six months "because my mom couldn't get out of bed. Postpartum depression." When baby Sandy returned to her mother, all seemed well for several years, and then her little brother was born—and once again her mother sunk into a depression although this time, she was not bedridden.

It was years later that I learned how impactful the early years of childhood and infancy can be and how the emotion we call shame sets down roots that continue to grow long after childhood is left behind.

Sandy was not my only client who talked about feelings of unworthiness and feeling like a fraud. There were many. In our culture, thousands feel something is wrong with them—that they aren't good enough, they don't belong, and they are somehow damaged. Despite anything friends, family, or therapists might say, they're caught in a nightmare of unworthiness that they cannot awaken from.

At that time, I had no idea Sandy's feelings were the fingerprint of shame. As I said, I thought it was poor self-esteem—I had yet to learn about childhood "relational" shame. This kind of shame originates from two sources. Relational shame is not the shame of doing things we regret—this is an insidious and poisonous set of false beliefs about ourselves that begins in childhood when the empathic attunement and emotional validation all children need is missing. It is also created by disparaging things parents and caretakers say to their children and the shame of blatant mistreatment and abuse. It is epidemic in proportion and perhaps one of the worst scourges a human can endure—a leakage through the drain hole of one's soul, as one author wrote.

This childhood shame can begin even before the baby has language, which explains why shame can be so deeply entrenched and often without words. Early childhood shame has no narrative and no memories of terrible things. Even as adults, the relational shame that began in childhood leaves us feeling broken, unworthy, unlovable, depressed, insufficient, and hopeless. It affects all parts of our lives—particularly our relationship with ourselves and with others. Nonetheless, it is also something we can overcome.

Healing shame

Early life relational shame is often not recognized, even by experienced therapists. For years, therapists, including myself, have failed to realize that many of the issues our clients consult us about—depression, anxiety, low self-esteem, eating disorders, suicidal thoughts, excessive anger, and failed relationships—*have early life shame at their core.* Because this early shame is seldom labeled accurately, it goes undetected and, therefore, untreated.

How can we heal this disguised shame if we haven't adequately identified it? *We can't.* As John Bradshaw, author of *Healing the Shame That Binds You (Bradshaw 1988),* said many years ago, "Shame was the unconscious demon I had never acknowledged. In naming shame, I began to have power over it." Chances are that you too have mislabeled and misunderstood the shame that fuels your unhappiness.

This is why understanding shame—your shame—is so critical. The feelings and thoughts of being broken and unworthy are not who you are, but rather, the sense you made of how you were treated as a child. When you recognize that your feelings of *not good enough* are the outcome of years of emotional and physical mistreatment (trauma), you can stop talking to your therapist about low self-esteem or reading self-help books on how to like yourself more and go straight to the root cause: childhood relational shame from an emotionally troubled childhood.

This is what this book is about and where the healing must begin.

Identifying my own unrecognized shame

When Sandy sat in front of me and asked me those questions, I had my own case of what I called "low self-esteem." (I never thought of it as a shame.) I too was caught in a trance of self-loathing that I could not shake. After decades as a psychotherapist, I was embarrassed that no amount of education, psychotherapy, self-help books, professional development, or words of reassurance from friends or family had healed my negative feelings about myself. And I was fed up with it. Like Sandy, I worried everyday—*What is wrong with me? Am I doomed to feel this way my whole frigging life?*

After thirty-five years of psychotherapy practice, I retired and moved to the coast, and yet, idyllic as that may sound, I felt frustrated that the easy, peaceful feelings I had hoped would be the hallmark of my retirement years were seldom available to me. Instead, I was painfully aware that my professional self was much more together than my personal self, and now that I no longer saw clients, my personal self was all I had. I was left with *her*. This engendered a strong motivation to focus on that personal self, hoping my professional self could help her as she had helped so many clients.

One morning, I was sitting quietly, coffee in hand, reflecting on a painful incident from my past. I had thought of it many times before because it was so humiliating. I was thirteen. It was an early summer evening, and we had company arriving, several couples we knew from our church. When I saw their car pull into the driveway, I noticed that the lawn sprinklers were on, and I could see water hitting the sidewalk where the guests would walk. So I went to the faucet and turned them off. Without warning, my stepfather came up from behind me, grabbed my shoulder from behind, turned his foot to the side, and kicked me in the butt—all while our company stood by watching. The kick was jarring, and a wave of humiliation washed over me. The company looked startled but did not say anything. Although I was seething with humiliation, I didn't say anything either and acted as though it hadn't happened. My reaction was so automatic—I didn't think of confronting my stepfather. Instead, I helped serve the guests, and when they left, I helped clean up the dishes.

It was a painful memory, but this time, as I recalled it, something caused me to look under the humiliation and anger I'd felt. That's where I discovered what I came to learn was *shame*. I felt the collapsed, appeasing sickness of shame as though it was happening again. The feeling of helplessness and acting as though nothing had happened was automatic and familiar. I felt weakness in my knees and my energy deflating.

It was a familiar feeling, yet I had never called it shame. In fact, if you asked me if I ever felt shame, I would have thought of the many shameful misdeeds from my past, such as betraying a friend and cheating on romantic partners, and answered "yes." But the kind of shame I felt that day wouldn't have come to mind. I thought shame was about things I had done, and I understood my despairing feelings and the omnipresent hateful self-talk the way most folks do—as low self-esteem, depression, and anxiety. It didn't enter my mind that toxic shame, the shame that takes over your mind and body, was at the core of these feelings.

My history of shame

I was almost an abortion. Born to a twenty-three-year-old divorced Mormon woman, my mother carried her shame of this out-of-wedlock pregnancy almost to her grave. Growing up, my mother never discussed anything about my father, and when I asked, she inferred that he was her ex-husband. When I graduated from college, we took a car trip together, and I pressed her to tell me why she had never talked to me about my father. She painfully told me a few things about her ex-husband, and then we had to pull off the road while she vomited and vomited. I thought she was carsick. Later I would learn the truth of why she was so sick.

Decades after that car trip, when my mother was in her mid-seventies and my stepfather was deceased, my aunt, who my mother lived with at the time, called to say my mother had something important to tell me. She said it was urgent. I arranged a flight, and a few days later, when I arrived at the apartment, my aunt sent my mother out of the room. Strange, I thought. Then my aunt told me that days earlier

my mother had come out of a meeting with her bishop crying and devastated. "Her first husband is not your father,
and she tried to get an abortion," is all I heard my aunt say. I
did not say anything to my mother when she returned to the
room. The information was too raw, and I felt sick inside.

I was in my mid-fifties when I learned all this, and it felt
like an emotional earthquake. For months, I wrestled with
whether to ask my mother about this secret she had carried.
What good would it do? I reasoned. I had the information
I needed to make sense of what I had felt my whole life: my
mother never loved or wanted me. I never asked my aunt
about it again. And I never talked to my mother. Was I protecting her? I'm not sure, but looking back, I do not regret
my decision.

In my first eight years, my mother and I lived with my
grandmother on a small dairy farm in Idaho. However, I do
not remember my mother during those years, and if it weren't
for some photos, I would swear she hadn't lived there. I now
know why: she never bonded with me. My grandmother,
who raised eight of her own children, was kind and protective, and I loved her dearly.

When I was eight, my mother remarried, and I went to
live with her and my new stepfather in Seattle. They had five
children over the next seven years. I was the built-in babysit-
ter and extra housekeeper. It seemed that was all I did. My
stepfather, who had spent his formative years in the military,
fighting in World War II and the Korean War, ran the family like the military in which he had grown up. My mother,
overwhelmed and believing she should back her husband,
deferred to his militaristic way of treating all the children. I
felt little connection to either of them. I felt alone and without an ally.

At fifteen, my life changed for ever. I was babysitting for a neighbor when their phone rang. I answered it, and a woman's voice told me that while I didn't know her, she had some important things to say to me. The unfamiliar woman's voice warned me that juvenile authorities would be coming to my parents' home in the next few days to talk with them about an illegal relationship I was having with a woman eighteen years my senior. The caller advised me to tell my parents before their arrival. She also said my parents should inform the authorities that they would send me to a psychiatrist. The dread of telling my parents was so heavy that I could barely breathe. But somehow, I managed to contact a young couple I knew from the church and asked them to come to the house. "I have something to tell my parents, and I need you there."

The next evening, as all of us sat in our living room, I tried to tell my parents I was gay. Neither of them could understand what I was saying until I used the term "homosexual." My mother went pale, and my stepfather said to her, "This must have come from your side of the family. She's not my kid." That was in 1963 in Alabama.

Thankfully the psychiatrist I did see did not try to cure me. Instead, he did his best to normalize being gay, which did not dislodge my own self-contempt. But he gave me two significant gifts: he told me my stepfather was "difficult," which affirmed that his dislike of me was not all my fault. He also advised my parents that I needed to live somewhere else. For my senior year, I went to live with an aunt and uncle in Salt Lake City. I was very grateful to them.

As I got older, much of this history was forgotten and replaced by trying to survive. My emotions were a mess, and I felt unmoored and not good enough most of the time.

My behavior was that of a lost and untethered young adult. Perhaps you can relate.

I knew I needed help. I thought my education in mental health would help, but it only gave me more information to feel bad about. I tried five years of psychotherapy. I read endless self-help books and took self-empowerment seminars. I learned meditation and took antidepressants. But still, the self-loathing, the insecurity, and the belief that I was somehow deficient lingered. Perhaps you too have felt frustrated because you can't shake your troubled feelings of self-disdain. You may have tried other common "strategies" as well, like overworking, overeating, over-drinking, drugs, empty sex, and the distraction of personal dramas. Some of these behaviors can be temporarily helpful, but as you have no doubt realized, they don't dissolve those pervasive feelings of unhappiness and unworthiness. This is the power of shame. First, it disguises itself. Then it thrives undetected.

How do you heal?

"Know your enemy" is good advice. The more you know about toxic shame, the more you have the upper hand because knowledge is power. *Bruised Not Broken* can help you do just that. This book answers Sandy's questions, which are the questions of millions of others, including me: *"What's wrong with me? Why do I feel I'm not good enough? Why do I hate myself?"* Maybe these are your questions too. If so, the pages that follow are for you.

Toxic shame is like a talented ventriloquist. It tricks you into believing its assessments, comments, warnings, and ugly criticisms are accurate messages about who you really are. Shame has borrowed your voice and it holds the microphone. It's easy to believe the voices you hear are your own thoughts. The messages and all the physical sensations accompanying them are so familiar that you accept them as who you are. Fortunately, as you name shame and understand how it operates, you will no longer be at the mercy of these deadly lies. You will recognize it as shame-speak, and you will have a choice whether to passively accept its insults or reject it as not true.

When I finally named toxic shame as my demon, I realized how little I knew. Like most therapists, I had never had a graduate course on trauma-induced shame, and it was not a topic of postgraduate courses. Luckily, some of the experts in trauma therapy were beginning to discuss toxic shame in short online trainings, and there was now cutting-edge professional literature on trauma treatment, which included the topic of shame.

First, I studied the writings of the best therapists and researchers in trauma treatment. Next, I reviewed my experiences as a therapist to see if their views fit my professional and personal experiences. (They did.) Finally, I dutifully used the healing practices on myself, and gradually, I noticed my experiences of shame, and my shame-thoughts gradually become less formidable. I learned to identify shame's messages, and instead of passively accepting its demeaning barrage, I learned processes that helped shut down the assaulting shame-speak. I will teach you how to do this too.

I also saw that those raised in healthy families possessed antidotes that calmed and reassured them when they were lost or frightened. I knew that shame-raised children didn't have them and would need to develop them intentionally. What were they? I compiled a list based on questions and

answers with healthy, thriving friends and in-laws, and I
studied the literature. Then I practiced those specific antidotes—the ones I'll teach you. Gradually, I noticed that
my mind grew quieter. My body felt calmer. The cluster of
knots in my stomach was only there occasionally. One day,
I noticed that the demeaning shame voices in my head had
utterly stopped. Wow! That was something. Also, memories
of mistreatment and emotional trauma from my childhood
began to recede into the past. I could feel shame lifting. It
was incremental, with ups and downs, but I was determined,
and the progress was ongoing.

Yet I knew that something more needed to happen. When
I caught myself telling stories about my upbringing and feeling resentment and disdain for those who mistreated me, I
felt thrown back into old feelings and negative thoughts. I
wanted those experiences to be in the past. What could make
that happen?

I had read research regarding the psychological value
of forgiveness, and while I thought I had forgiven everyone
(*"I forgive them,"* I would tell myself), something lingered.
Maybe I really didn't know how to forgive. Reluctantly, I
began to consider forgiveness—not the version I associated
with Sunday school, where I had learned that God wanted
me to forgive, but a research-based process, which I'll teach
you. I wanted to be free of resentment, anger, and hate.
Then I tackled self-forgiveness, the difficult acceptance that
I'm more than my worst behavior.

Somewhere along this journey, most unexpectedly, I
started to hear what I called the still, small voice of Spirit,
and I began to see myself in a more loving light. I did not
know that this voice was a compassionate part of myself,
a presence we all possess, even if we don't believe in it. I

discovered that when shame begins to lift and our inner shame voices become quiet, we can all experience this compassionate voice. It is our birthright.

The structure of this book

Bruised Not Broken is divided into three parts.

Part 1 focuses on learning how toxic shame is trauma-induced within the parent-child relationship and how many widespread parenting practices perpetuate this kind of shame. However, not all trauma-induced toxic shame stems from what was done to you. Some of the earliest and most impactful wounding is from the trauma of what is missing.

Part 2 explains what you can do to heal, both the self-shaming habits you need to stop and the emotional and physical antidotes you must cultivate and use to heal your wounds and protect you in the future. You'll learn why you sometimes feel and act in ways you don't understand, as if you were taken over by an alien part of yourself. Learning how to work with those "alien" wounded parts of yourself that are still stuck in trauma is central to your healing.

Part 3 introduces the power of forgiveness as a choice you can make to leave your past in the past. This section explores the myths and misunderstandings about forgiveness—(forget and forgive is one of them)—that often stop us from even exploring it. Finally, we'll look at self-forgiveness, which is hard to give ourselves. We were not raised knowing our mistakes and actions are not who we are.

Each chapter revolves around the central premise that toxic, relational shame can be healed when we understand where it came from, how it works, and how we can give ourselves the emotional medicine to heal it. As you will see, you have the power to heal your shame.

The theories and suggestions I describe on these pages are supported by science and research. They also draw from my own healing experiences and my insights as a psycho-therapist for many years, specializing in treating people who were emotionally and physically abused as children. The healing suggestions I offer are meant to be augmented by everything you already know and will learn as you pursue your healing.

I have accompanied many on their healing journey, and now I want to accompany you. I want you to experience the healing I have found. As you read this book, I hope you'll sense that I'm there, walking with you every step of the way. *I am your ally.*

My blessing for you

May you be free of shame's poison.
May your thoughts of unworthiness drop from you like a feather drops from a bird in flight.
May your heart glow with love for yourself and others.
May forgiveness be your daily bread.
May your words, your walk, your actions reflect who you really are:
A worthy, beautiful being who deserves to be free of suffering.

Let's begin.

1

Making Sense of Shame

When a client feels overwhelmed with self-loathing, I'll name what's happening as "Shame" and I'll call it an enemy, a force bigger than she is at the moment, but not the truth about who she is.

—Patricia DeYoung

Shame lurks in the shadows of our minds as an unwelcome guest, rarely spoken of but deeply felt. Shame is unique and elusive. But it's definitely not subtle. We all know how it feels. It is the sickness in the pit of our stomach, the worry that our brokenness will be discovered. It is the only emotion that makes us feel bad about ourselves. "Shame is a much more powerful and pervasive problem than most of us realize, a terrible life-long affliction." (DeYoung 2015)

Shame is complex. Sometimes, it is confused with guilt or humiliation. It is believed to be adaptive as well as destructive. Theorists suggest that shame may have played a crucial role in early human history by promoting cooperation and reducing aggression within social groups. They suggest that early humans lacked the brain development to self-regulate their aggression and had little capacity to care for each other. Shaming from an external source allowed our ancestors to form clans and groups that enhanced their odds of survival. But modern humans have a brain that gives them the capacity to cooperate and feel compassion for others. They don't need an outside source. Those feelings that make up the best of being human now come from within themselves, and when they are shamed by others and made to feel bad about themselves, it is destructive in ways that affect every part of their lives. This book is about how destructive shame can be.

How shame can begin in childhood

Humiliating shaming, such as verbal, physical, and sexual abuse, including overly harsh parenting, is a soul-murdering shame. But what we often fail to realize is that being ignored and emotionally lonely is traumatic too. Being without a significant other who delights in your presence is also shaming. We recognize this as shame because of how it leads to feelings of not good enough, not worthy, and not lovable … the fingerprints of shame. It is behind many of the issues that lead clients to seek psychotherapy.

"Chronic shame can feel like a one-person failing caused by one's own negative thinking and low self-esteem. But in fact, shame is relational. A chronic sense of being disconnected from those we count on becomes a profound sense of isolation, which in turn leads to despair and unworthiness." (DeYoung 2015)

When you observe a four- or five-month-old child, it is easy to see how confident and self-assured they feel. When they want comfort or attention, when they want to be fed or their diaper changed, they do not hesitate to let you know. Their cries are unapologetic demands for what they need and want. "Give this to me now." Even as they smile and tease, they do so with the confidence that they are lovable and winsome. What happens to that confidence, to that self-assured knowledge that they deserve love and attention?

What is relational shame?

Imagine having a conversation with someone significant in your life and pouring out an experience you've had that frightened and upset you. You want comfort and understanding. Imagine that after listening briefly, this friend begins to tell you a story from their own life of something scary that happened to them, suggesting that what happened to you couldn't have been that bad. And then, without a pause, adds that maybe you're making too big of a deal of it.

How do you feel? Stunned. Hurt and angry. Dismissed. But you may also feel defeated, deflated, and empty. Your posture slumps, and you become confused. You feel weak. This is a shame attack. Later, you find yourself wondering if they had a point. Maybe you do make too big a deal of things. Shame creeps into your thoughts about yourself. It confuses you and keeps you off balance.

Now imagine a young baby that has awoken from a nap and cries out for its mother. He is eagerly anticipating a reunion that is happy and engaging. But what if, instead, his mother arrives with a frustrated expression and says something he can't understand, but her voice is cold and harsh? She doesn't look at him. As she picks him up, her behavior is rough and robotic. How does the baby feel? Frightened, threatened, unsafe.

The messaging they get from their caretakers, whether verbal, behavioral, or emotional, often blames the child for the parent's mistreatment. "I just changed you. What do you need now? If you'd stop spilling things … If you'd quit your whining … If you weren't so bad …!"

Relational shame is most damaging when we are children. Our parents or primary caretakers are often "well-meaning but fragile, wounded parents." (DeYoung 2015) Many struggle not only with their own emotional well-being but also with economic pressures and a lack of support from family or friends. Maybe the parents themselves were raised by older siblings or left to raise themselves, and while they may not have liked those arrangements, so much of what we do as parents reflects how we were raised. They may be a single parent, but even a two-parent family does not ensure that a child will get emotional nurturing. Often, our idea of raising children doesn't recognize how critical it is for them to have a reliable emotional connection with at least one caretaker.

A child formulates everything they feel about themselves based on how their caretakers feel about them, and they know this at a very early age, around two, if not earlier. How could it be otherwise? The emotional and physical feedback from a child's primary caretaker becomes the basis for a child's self-esteem, self-concept, and physical and emotional well-being.

For generations, parents have used shaming to shape behavior and, especially, to deter misbehavior. Shaming has historically been an acceptable parenting practice that originated when children were thought to be born full of evil and sin, like wild animals that needed to be broken. Now we know that shaming is like using a hammer when a slight nudge will do. It is a cruel message that you are bad for what you do or what you want. Think about what a blow this must be to the child who comes into life full of confidence and joy. When frequent messages of disapproval and disdain are focused on a child, their fragile self-confidence is crushed, and inside, they no longer feel good about themselves. Instead, when their feelings of confidence and being lovable are carved down to nothing, they feel bad, and pleasing the adult on whom they depend for survival becomes their focus. They submit, collapse, and try to appease the invalidating parent. Sadly, the child focuses not on enjoying their new life, but on being acceptable. The fear of being physically and, most importantly, emotionally abandoned surges through their nervous system. Being acceptable eventually becomes their most compelling emotional issue.

Shame is a survival response that you have no conscious control over

All mammals, from the time of birth, have a set of automatic, unconscious survival responses that are set in motion by the nervous system when a significant threat is sensed. These are activated involuntarily, which is a crucial point.

There are five innate survival responses:

1. Cry out for help and safety.
2. Fight and try to overcome an oppressor.
3. Flight—flee, run away.
4. Freeze and play dead.
5. Submit–collapse–appease.

This fifth survival response is shame. We do not consciously choose a response when threatened. Instead, the nervous system instantaneously assesses which of the five responses is best for our survival. These are the automatic responses initiated by the central nervous system; we act without thinking.

Here is a brief look at how this works. When you are threatened or feel unsafe, your nervous system will first consider crying out for help. But if no one comes to your aid, or you're in immediate danger, it then reverts to fight. *Can I overpower the person who's threatening to hurt me and then get away?* If the answer is "yes," you will fight.

But if you're a helpless child or an overpowered adult who can't fight, your nervous system will next assess: *Can I flee? Can I run away?* When that answer is "no," such as when a child lives with a scary or neglectful parent or when an adult is pinned down and raped, the nervous system will assess: *Can I play dead or freeze and thereby escape danger?*

Finally, when even that choice isn't safe, the nervous system will choose the response of last resort: *Can I collapse, appease, submit, and thereby be safe?* This is the shame response—the response when there are no other options. Because both the freeze and collapse–appease–submit put the brakes on your energy and shift the body into a deactivated state, your body goes limp, your behavior becomes robotic, you may appear to be in a daze (dissociated), and you become compliant and non-combative.

I want to emphasize that the shame survival response of submit–collapse–appease behavior is a last resort, an automatic response to overwhelming, threatening, or endangering situations.

When a child experiences repeated emotional abandonment, such as when a parent will not look at the child or respond to them, the nervous system is predisposed to choose the submit–collapse–appease response. In a shame state, a child will seek to please and appease and try to figure out how to become more acceptable, hoping the parent will connect with them emotionally. *How can I behave so my mother will take care of me and want to be with me?* The child instinctively tries to make themselves as appealing as possible. If the parent is emotionally absent or rejection is frequent, the child will unconsciously translate this into feeling *I must be unworthy of my mother's love; something is wrong with me*. How else could a child interrupt the parent's behavior?

Over time, if the shame response is triggered repeatedly because of abuse, neglect, abandonment, or toxic experiences, the child will become shame-prone. This means collapse–submit–appease will become a chronic response when the child senses a threat. The ability to tolerate some threat without going into a survival response is diminished, and the child's nervous system will initiate the shame response in situations where others may not feel threatened. This is referred to as the window of tolerance, and the less secure and connected we felt to our caretaker, the smaller the window. This propensity to feel shame when even a tiny threat is sensed (someone yawns while we're talking to them) persists into adulthood. It is possible, however, to widen this window, and the chapter on healing offers some practices.

Adults experience the shame response as well. In instances of physical trauma (being hit, shot, slapped, raped, beaten) or emotional abuse (experiencing humiliation, intimidation, sadistic sarcasm, gaslighting), the submit–collapse–appease is often a survival choice when one must be nonthreatening or submissive to the aggressor. This lessens the risk of further injury—whether for an adult or a child. In this way, shame is an adaptive response to threat, not a pathological or cowardly response. It's a submission to someone or something stronger, bigger, meaner, or life-threatening. We don't say to ourselves, *Submission would be the best choice here.* Instead, we feel the sudden sinking of our energy—one of the markers that the nervous system is downregulating into the shame response—and our thinking and verbal skills go offline. We cooperate, we collapse, and we appease.

How shame feels in our body

To submit–collapse–appease, our physiology goes from being highly activated (cry out, fight, flee) to suddenly losing energy. Physically, this is a terrible feeling. It's the same awful feeling we have as adults when we experience a sick, sinking feeling that overcomes us, leaving us drained, powerless, and queasy. "Shame is felt as an inner torment, a sickness of the soul." (Schore 2015)

This survival-based shame response affects our breathing, the stomach, kidneys, and intestines. Our heart rate plunges, we struggle to breathe, and our stomach is tied in knots. Or as Van der Kolk says, "The bowels empty too quickly, literally scaring the shit out of us. This is the point at which we collapse and move into the appease-please response known as shame." (Van der Kolk 2014)

It's important to remember that the shame response of submit–collapse–appease is an automatic, instinctive choice that we have no control over. Think about that for a minute. This means you didn't choose to submit or go along with your abuser. It means you had no choice when you became compliant and couldn't stick up for yourself. It means when you were emotionally degraded or humiliated, you didn't choose to appease. Your autonomic nervous system chose for you.

How shame turns chronic and toxic

Children are particularly vulnerable to the shame response because they are entirely dependent on adults and have so few survival options. Frequent and prolonged exposure to physically or emotionally upsetting or terrifying experiences during the critical times of infancy and childhood causes the shame response to stay activated in the nervous system. When this happens, it becomes chronic and toxic. This may look like poor self-esteem. But shame is a response to trauma. It is a survival strategy, not low self-esteem.

It's important to note that not every shame response turns toxic. For example, when a mother is usually responsive to her baby's cries for help or connection, *infrequent* absences aren't traumatic enough to cause chronic shame, even though they may be temporarily painful emotionally. If the parenting figure lovingly repairs the attachment bond by comforting and soothing her child, the emotional attachment is reestablished, and the child reconnects and feels safe again.

What causes something to be traumatic?

What qualifies as traumatic depends on the age of the child, temperament, the relationship of the offender to the child, and the specific threat. When the emotion of an experience—terrifying fear, for example—is too overwhelming for the child's brain and nervous system to process and move beyond, that is traumatic. A child needs support and comfort to work through and calm their nervous system from huge emotional surges. Consider, for example, the toddler who accidentally spills her milk. Her angry father hits her, scolds her, and then ignores her pleas for comfort. Consider the eight-year-old boy who tells his father, "I don't have to," and is stripped down and spanked (beaten) with a paddle. While these examples are about physical mistreatment and abuse, they are also about emotional trauma. What does the child feel? *I am not loved or cherished. I do not feel safe. My parents are a danger to me. I live in an unsafe, harsh world with no one to rely on.* This is trauma.

What is considered trauma has broadened as our understanding of the significance of emotional distress evolved. In the past, professionals used the term traumatic to describe certain events. For example, being locked in a closet for hours is traumatic to a child. But now, we know it isn't just the physical acts, but also the level of emotional trauma that matters. As Gabor Maté (Maté 2023), an expert on trauma treatment, noted, "Trauma isn't simply what happens to us. It's what goes on inside us." Trauma is a wound that occurs inside us, a wound that leads to a belief that *I'm not worthy because if I were worthy, this bad thing wouldn't be happening to me.* Not worthy of love, protection, or belonging—these are the wounds of trauma and the feelings of shame.

Some traumas are not as obvious as others. Being mocked by your parents when you're distressed, being belittled for your efforts, or being ignored or repeatedly called "stupid" are all traumatic. The parent on whom the child's life depends is experienced as unsafe and frightening. The child feels alone and threatened, and that sets off survival alarms. When parents fight in front of their child, it scares their child. When parents are emotionally unavailable due to excessive stress, drug use, mental illness, and neglect, the child feels alone, threatened, and without protection and safety. This is traumatic.

There is also a kind of threat we likely would not label as a threat at all. When I first encountered a client with this kind of childhood experience, I didn't understand that what looked like a mother's deep caring was actually something very different. In her book *Healing Your Emotional Self* (Engel 2006), Beverly Engel describes "over-mothering," also known as "smothering." As Engel describes it, when a mother or primary caretaker routinely over-protects and interferes with a child's normal need to be an independent and separate little person, the child's natural development is obstructed. This thwarts the child's critical development toward increased self-reliance and independence. For example, consider the mother who habitually insists on feeding her seven-year-old daughter rather than encouraging self-sufficiency. It may also be over-mothering when she insists on driving her ten-year-old son to school "for safety reasons" when he wants to walk with his friends. The caretaker who monitors her child's every move communicates to the child that they are not safe without her.

Too often, when this child tries to exert her own will with actions such as refusing to be fed, the smothering mother feels rejected, shows frustration, and may become angry. But the child's acts of "willfulness" are a necessary step towards developing a separate self. In her coldness and rejection, the mother is essentially telling the daughter, "You need me to take care of you because you are not capable yourself." Contrary to the truth, the child may be accused of being selfish and non-appreciative for wanting independence. The more significant message is that she is bad when she tries to follow her natural urge for more independence and self-reliance. This is traumatic for any child. Every child needs their parents to support and encourage their unfolding, little, separate self. When this is missing or discouraged, even punished, this is the shame of smothering.

Understanding the response of submit–collapse–appease in adults

As adults, when we reflect on how we responded to a threatening situation, we often feel ashamed of our collapse-submit–appease responses. We haven't understood that this response is our nervous system's best attempt to keep us from being hurt. Again, our rational mind doesn't make the decision to respond in this way. Instead, the rational part of our brain mind is disabled. We don't think; we respond instinctively. Let me repeat this. We don't think, because our thinking brain is disabled. When we accept this fact, which has been proven repeatedly through brain imaging, we can begin to have self-compassion for some of the behaviors for which we've harshly judged ourselves.

One of my adult clients was raped while on vacation in Miami. As we discussed her terrifying experience, her biggest question was, "Why didn't I run? Why didn't I fight?" But when I asked her if she could remember what she was thinking while being attacked, her response was, "All I kept thinking was 'stay alive, stay alive.'" When she learned that she couldn't choose to run or fight because her survival brain had taken over, she began to accept that she'd had no choice. Under threat for survival, her nervous system chose the survival response it assessed as safest: collapse–appease–submit.

Consider, too, the situation of my client Susan, who was placed in foster care at age twelve when her single mother was convicted of armed robbery and narcotics possession. As a child, Susan was often left for days to fend for herself while her mother was on a drug binge. She was sometimes removed from her mother's custody but always returned within a few months. When her mother was sent to prison, she was placed in foster care and moved from one foster home to another before finally being placed with an aunt and uncle. On the surface, this appeared great: family, a swimming pool, a friendly aunt who worked as a CPA, and an uncle who worked part-time as a mechanic. But all was not well.

Too often, when Susan came home from school, she opened the front door and encountered a drunk uncle. At first, when he wanted her to sit beside him and talk about her day and her friends, she liked his attention. All humans, especially children, have an inborn need for attention, to be valued, and to get approval. It was a feeling she had longed for. So she readily agreed. She enjoyed the feeling of some- one being interested in her, but, sadly, her uncle began making sexual advances toward her. She was terrified and felt betrayed. Perhaps the worst part was that she felt her body responding. Her confusion was consuming. She knew it was wrong and wanted to get away. Ashamed and trapped, she tried harder to resist, but he became more aggressive. Finally, he threatened to return her to foster care and blamed her for seducing him.

Years later, when I first met Susan, she was ashamed and full of self-hate. "How could I have just gone along with that stuff for so long?" she asked. "What the hell was wrong with me? Why did I wait so long to run away?" But when she learned about our instinctive survival responses to danger, her attitude toward herself began to soften. "Understanding the collapse-appease-submit response helps me release a lot of shame," she said. "I wondered why I would just go along with it. It made me feel horrible that sometimes it felt good. How dirty and weird could I be? Now, I understand that his threats and abuse set off a survival response—probably one I had experienced many times with my mom's neglect and rejection. It was all horrible."

Susan's young nervous system made the submit–col- lapse–appease choice after determining that she had no other choice. But by the time she was fifteen, her mind had made a different choice, and she ran away.

"Unfortunately," Susan told me, "I still use collapse– submit–appease whenever there is lots of conflict. When someone gets angry with me, I get scared, and it's like I can't help it. I wish I could tell myself to stand up, to grow a spine, because then I don't think I'd feel so cowardly. Now I see that this response was, as you have said, a well-learned survival response, and whenever situations feel threatening, my nervous system acts as though it's life-threatening. Understanding this helps me feel some compassion for myself and less broken. I know how it works and I can choose to change that response. I have more choices now."

Our culture hasn't understood that survival shame is a response we have no control over. Yet, ironically, not speaking up, not fighting, not running away, not seeking help, and keeping our misery a secret is a survival response that may have saved us. Stephen Porges, an expert on survival strategies for trauma and author of *The Polyvagal Response* (Porges 2011), wrote, "Appeasement is a very skillful neurobiological strategy of survival which provides sufficient clues to the aggressor to make the aggressor believe that you are on board. Appeasement is a valiant attempt that the nervous system makes to enable us to navigate a complex situation. Because if there is not appeasement, there is injury on the other side of the equation." This is our terrible bargain for safety. The other options would only lead to more significant harm.

Porges' compassionate insights can help us understand that appeasement is an adaptive survival response undertaken by a resilient mind and nervous system. This realization is freeing and helps counter "Why didn't you stick up for yourself? Why weren't you more assertive?" We can feel grateful for how adaptive we were, and we can think of our behaviors differently—without judgment and eventually compassion. We are ingenious survivors.

The Value of a Notebook

How can we best capture our insights and progress as we heal? Having a dedicated notebook that you can write in serves as a way to explore your thoughts and feelings more deeply and to remind you of what you have discovered. Merely thinking about your insights or personal revelations is a sure way to forget them. I suggest you find a notebook and chronicle the process of getting to know yourself better. You can then draw on it to remind yourself of how you're healing, the progress you're making, and the growing healthy relationship you are building with yourself. When we are healing, it is often difficult to see our progress. Mostly we know about our progress through hindsight.

Chapter Takeaways

1. Shame is an automatic survival response triggered when an individual's central nervous system perceives overwhelming fear or danger.
2. The shame response of collapse–submit–appease can become chronic and toxic if the shame response is frequent and prolonged.
3. Shame may have played a crucial role in early human history by promoting cooperation and reducing aggression within social groups. But modern humans have the capacity to think of others and cooperate without being shamed. Shaming is a demoralizing affront.

4. Trauma is not about what happened to you but how it affected you.

5. Despite the common use of shaming in parenting, shaming is NOT an effective way to socialize or deter wrongdoing.

Reflection Question

Drawing on the understanding that shame is an automatic, instinctive response to threat, can you identify situations in your past where you harshly judged yourself for submitting or appeasing in the face of conflict or danger? How does recognizing these responses as survival strategies impact your self-perception and self-compassion?

2

The Shame of What Was Done and What Was Missing

Over the years, our research team has repeatedly found that chronic emotional abuse and neglect can be just as devastating as physical abuse and sexual molestation.

—Bessel van der Kolk

Reflecting on your childhood, you may not recall anything you would label "abusive." Searching through your childhood memory bank, you may assume you survived unscathed. But not all incidents that trigger the survival response of shame are sexual or physical abuse. Sarcastic put-downs, name-calling, unfavorable comparisons to other kids or siblings, mocking, cruel teasing, and scathing criticism are also abusive experiences.

But there is also another source of shame: the shame of what was missing. This is the shame of emotional neglect, rejection, emotional abandonment, and oppressive smothering we discussed in the previous chapter. It doesn't matter whether it was intentional or unintentional. Since we typically don't label these experiences as abuse, they often aren't recognized as such, but these are indeed abuse. Deprivation of the emotional connection and responsiveness that are critical to children's well-being triggers the survival response of shame. To be healthy, just as the physical body relies on consistent, reliable healthy food, so the emotional body, known as the self, requires consistent, reliable emotional engagement.

Healthy emotional development requires the *undivided* attention and the warm emotional *engagement* of caretakers. A baby's brain growth and emotional well-being require the caretakers' smiles, cooing, cajoling, kind tones, and mutual eye contact. Reliable and consistent emotional engagement lays down brain circuits of safety and well-being in the new little human. When caretakers mimic the baby's facial expressions, engage in long moments of mutual gazing, playfully tickle, and follow the lead of the child's antics, they provide the nourishment the baby's brain and emotional well-being require. It feeds the fragile emotional "body" known as the sense of self.

Emotional engagement requires more than just being present. It isn't enough to feed and clothe a child and set them up in front of a TV, iPad, or smartphone. Likewise, when the parent is texting or checking social media while holding their baby, they aren't connected in a way that provides the emotional nourishment the child needs. Think about how it feels to you as an adult when you're trying to engage with someone who is constantly monitoring their texts or skimming through Instagram. Such experiences leave even an adult feeling disconnected and unimportant. Repeated experiences of this kind of "benign" neglect are devastating for a child because all children require the emotional connection of a reliable caretaker for a healthy brain and emotional well-being.

The harm done to the cognitive and emotional brain doesn't just go away as we get older. Van der Kolk cites a study about the long-term effects of insufficient or abusive mothering. For thirty years beginning in 1975, researcher Alan Sroufe and colleagues followed 180 children and their families, starting before the children were born and continuing to when they reached age twenty-eight. His findings were striking. Sroufe and colleagues concluded that more important than the mother's personality, the child's temperament, or the child's IQ, the *most significant* predictor of whether the child would develop serious behavioral problems was the nature of the parent–child relationship and how loveable the mothers rated their child at age two.

By age two, as Sroufe and others note, a child knows how the important people in her life feel about her, and this is how she will feel about herself. "Since the earliest period of our life was preverbal, everything depended on emotional interaction. Without someone to reflect our emotions, we had no way of knowing who we are." (Tangney and Dearing 2002)

Physical comfort isn't enough

Before the 1960s and going back decades, if not centuries, many parents and even psychologists downplayed the role of emotional needs in early childhood development. It's hard to believe, but many erroneously thought a baby sought out and wanted to be connected to its caretaker because she was the food source. We have not always understood the primacy of emotional nurturing in child–parent relationships. Quite the contrary, many child-rearing principles passed on through the generations saw the goal of parenting as providing food and clothing and raising a compliant child. A child's emotional well-being was not on the radar.

An American psychologist named Harry Harlow argued that the focus on compliance overlooked the importance of comfort, companionship, and love in promoting healthy development. His now famous experiments confirmed this. In his experiments, conducted in the 1950s, he separated a baby rhesus monkey from its mother and raised it in a cage with two surrogate "mothers" made of wire. One wire mother had a bottle attached to her, and another was wrapped in foam rubber and terry cloth with no bottle. Watson observed that as soon as the infant monkey finished bottle feeding, it abandoned the wire monkey with the bottle and clung to the soft cloth wire mother that held no bottle.

However, the cloth monkey wasn't an adequate substitute to provide the emotional-social needs of the little monkey. Rhesus monkeys are like humans in their need for intimate physical contact with mothers who respond to their emotional and physical needs. Not surprisingly, when the socially isolated monkey grew older, it had severe emotional and behavioral problems. Its early emotional deprivation precluded it from having the skills and inner confidence needed to interact successfully with its peers or social group. The little monkey was terrified.

This may seem like an extreme example that's less applicable to children, but the implications are sobering. Both monkeys and children require emotional engagement. Food or the mere presence of an adult isn't enough.

Still Face experiments

The Still Face experiments conducted in the 1970s by Harvard psychologist Dr. Edward Tronick advanced our understanding of the importance of emotional engagement. He showed that children as young as a few months old were devastated when they were emotionally cut off from their parents. He also showed how the shame response can be triggered even when the parent is present.

Tronick's experiments are available on YouTube, and I highly recommend watching them. You can find them with the prompt "Still Face Experiment." (Tronick n.d.) In the first segment, a mother warmly engages with her one-year-old girl sitting in a baby's highchair. Both are smiling and laughing. As the baby points to the cinematographer, the mother looks, too. Next, the mother tickles her daughter's foot, and the baby responds with joyful giggles. They're both enjoying each other and enlivened by the dance of their playful exchanges.

In the next segment, the mother, as instructed by the researcher, turns her face away. Moments later, the mother turns back to face the little girl, and while maintaining eye contact, her face is completely expressionless. Startled, we see confusion and fear on the baby's face. Trying to renew the emotional connection with the mother, the baby begins repeating the behaviors that worked previously: she laughs, points to the cinematographer, and then forlornly reaches out her little arms. She fusses and squirms. But the mother's face remains unmoved.

The baby begins to cry. Then, she leans back in her chair and shrieks. The mother's face remains unchanged. After a few more futile attempts, the little girl twists her body and faces away from the mother. Finally, she stops trying to engage. She gives up, and her body begins to slump. Her crying becomes quieter, more plaintive, and more hopeless. Then, she's silent. At this point, the mother smiles and reaches out. The baby looks quizzically at her mother and smiles cautiously. She appears relieved but uncertain. Finally, she reaches out to the mother's outstretched arms, her little face brightens, and she cuddles into the mother.

For several years, Tronick and his students conducted many of these experiments, which are not allowed today. In experiment after experiment with children ranging from infants to young children, all reacted in the same way. After the initial ramped-up attempts to regain the connection with the mother came "the cry for help" survival response: the child's face saddens, followed by cries and pleas. Sometimes, there are angry shrieks—the "fight" response—and when the mother's face doesn't respond, they turn away—"flight." Then the child's energy downregulates, and their body slumps—"submit–collapse–appease." This physiological–emotional sequence is what shame looks like.

Tronick describes this sequence as "the good, bad, and ugly." The good, he says, is what all parents do. They're disengaged for short periods of time and then re-engage emotionally and physically. The bad is when the baby's emotional needs are ignored more frequently and for extended periods before the parent finally re-engages. The ugly is when the baby experiences prolonged emotional disengagement, and there is no re-engagement. "They are stuck," Tronick says. This stuck experience is what we mean by chronic shame. "People did not think infants could engage in social interactions. But his experiments showed that children as young as months old are extremely responsive to the emotions and the reactivity and social interactions that they get from the world around them."

More recently, Allan Schore, a respected neuropsychologist on the clinical faculty at the UCLA School of Medicine, studied the brains of five-month-old infants while they briefly looked at their blank-faced mothers. In these EEG studies, the emotional brain region of the baby, which develops before the cognitive brain, "matched the rhythmic structures of the mother's emotional brain state." What does this say about babies raised by depressed, dissociated, overwhelmed, preoccupied, or addicted caretakers? Schore concluded that if this is a frequent or ongoing experience, the results can be emotional "instability, inefficient stress tolerance, memory impairment, psychosomatic disorders, and dissociative disturbances." (Schore 2015)

The importance of identifying unrecognized shame

The abuse of emotional rejection, humiliation, and ignoring are examples of unrecognized trauma which leads to shame. It's unrecognized because these patterns of behavior are seldom called "traumatic." The symptoms of unrecognized shame are also incredibly challenging for us to identify and understand in ourselves, particularly when the abuse happened before we had language. Many of my clients didn't remember blatant abuse and couldn't understand why they felt "not good enough," "defective," and "broken." They were puzzled because there were no memories of beatings or being locked in a closet, but again, they didn't know about the trauma of what was missing.

The terror of emotional neglect in early childhood lives in our bodies as sensations, often experienced as anxiety and depression, are without words. This terror was embedded in our nonverbal brain. It is challenging to access because there were no words, but nonetheless, a powerful influence on how we felt as children and how we came to feel as adults. These body sensations, feelings of anxiety or depression, thoughts of being worthless and damaged live in us without a verbal narrative. When we do acquire language by age two or three, we will give words to these previously wordless feelings, such as "bad girl," "stupid boy," and, later, "worthless, not good enough, defective." These awful feelings over time will morph into an identity of how we feel about ourselves—*I am not good enough*—and even self-hate. "Most of us who hate ourselves are not aware of doing so. It is the default setting of our personality." *(The School of Life* 2019)

My client, Jessie, came to see me because of unrelenting depression and poor self-esteem. She had no memories of blatant abuse, but she did remember that as a young child, she frequently didn't know where her mother was and that her sister, four years older, was her caretaker. Several family photos showed Jessie sitting alone in a playpen. One happy photo was of Jessie dancing in the living room with her sister. But there were many memories of getting up for school with no parents present and returning home on her bike to a house with only her sister. Jessie didn't know why her mother was absent, but she did know that she felt unwanted, empty, and resoundingly not good enough. She suffered from the shame of what was missing.

Hello, my name is "worthless"

Tragically, children don't know that they could never be "good enough" to unaccepting, confused, overwhelmed, addicted, immature, inadequate, or cruel parents. As children, we think it's our fault that we feel like an emotional orphan. Janina Fisher, an expert in trauma treatment, observed that children would rather blame themselves for their parent's rejection, neglect, or cruelty than believe they live in a world where they have no allies or reliable person with whom they can find safety.

Consider, for example, a young boy I witnessed shopping with his father in a grocery store over the winter holidays. It was late in the day, and the aisles were jammed. The store had stacked extra merchandise in the aisles, making it almost impossible to navigate. The boy, about age ten, was trying to maneuver his large cart through this maze. Repeatedly, his father said in a demeaning tone, "I told you to stay with me. What are you doing? Can't you think? Pay attention!" I became upset when I heard this, and although the boy was clearly hurt, he answered politely and did his best. I was in a quandary about whether I should say anything. Finally, when the father snapped, "Can't you do anything right?" I waited until the man was out of earshot and said to the boy, "It's so crowded in here that no one can keep up with anyone. You're doing just fine." He smiled shyly. But I knew his father's demeaning messages would be deeply embedded into his sense of self. He would absorb the messages of *not good enough* and *stupid*, and nothing I could say would change that.

In time, this boy may reflect back on his life from an adult perspective and wonder why he didn't stick up for himself when his father was so harsh and critical. He may look at his younger self and feel ashamed that he seemed to go along and try to please his father. I hope someone will tell him about the collapse–appease–submit survival response and suggest that his nervous system made a wise choice to keep him from further harm and as emotionally connected to his father as possible. Later, he will have other options, but not at ten years old.

The only thing wrong with those of us who suffer toxic shame is that some terrible things happened to us. We were deprived of emotional safety and connection, love, and acceptance. Yes, it hurt us, and we may still suffer from that cruelty, but as you'll see, it didn't break us. Bruised but not broken, we can take steps now as adults to challenge the ugly shame messages that have invaded our inner dialogues.

Chapter Takeaways

1. Chronic emotional abuse and neglect can be just as damaging as physical and sexual abuse.
2. Experiences such as sarcastic put-downs, name-calling, and emotional abandonment are examples of what was done to us.
3. Babies and children require consistent emotional engagement from their caretakers. Merely being physically present is not sufficient. When that is missing, it becomes the shame of what was missing.
4. A loving and emotionally responsive connection between parent and infant is vital for a child's self-worth and self-esteem.

5. Emotional rejection, humiliation, and ignoring are examples of unrecognized abuse that can be challenging to identify because it is seldom seen as abuse.

Reflection Question

Reflecting on the discussion of emotional neglect, can you understand how "what was missing" may have been a bigger factor in your childhood than you previously realized? How has this insight helped you understand your feelings of unworthiness, not good enough, broken?

3

Shame-Speak: The Ventriloquist in Our Heads

Shame's a very powerful emotion because of the way it sneaks up and just takes over a person's organism from the inside.

—Peter Levine

I used to think the self-deprecating statements that came out of my mouth were harmless—unpleasant for others to hear perhaps, but still harmless. "How stupid can you be?" I'd mutter when I made a mistake. Or when I sent an email and later discovered a word was missing, "What an idiot! What's wrong with you, stupid?" Sometimes I'd just hurl such labels as "lame," "f—k-up," "weird," or "hopeless." And there was always the omnipresent "sorry," which I repeated at the beginning and end of almost all my statements. "I'm sorry, but I'd like Mexican food for dinner." "I'm sorry, but can I ask you to spell his name." In my emotional lexicon, "I'm sorry" meant "I'm a sorry person. I know I'm unworthy. I'm sorry I'm such a bother."

There are other shame-speak phrases like "I'm too needy," "I'm too sensitive," "I'm too emotional," "I'm too shy," "I talk too much," and "I'm too nervous and insecure." There are also the ones like "I'm not bright enough," "I'm not funny enough," and "I'm not cute enough … thin enough … pretty enough." "I'm not important." "I don't fit in." And sometimes it's just the thought, "I can't do anything right."

All of these statements reflect shame's hallmark messages: *I'm broken, flawed, not good enough, incapable, defective, and therefore unlovable.*

Hearing these false self-assessments in our mind is debilitating, but I didn't know that every time I repeated these putdowns, I perpetuated my shame. Unbeknownst to me, I kept my shame alive by thoughtlessly and habitually telling myself the things shame had put into my head. *Our minds do not know the difference between what others say to us and what we say to ourselves.* These words weren't harmless; they were self-assaulting, corrosive, and, worst of all, I thought they were true.. For example, when I called myself stupid because I had called someone the wrong name, I thought only a stupid person would make such a mistake. I didn't argue with this shame-speak I'd heard in my head, nor did I try to defend myself. Even as an adult, the part of me that believed "stupid" to be true was more influential and powerful than I ever imagined.

When I began to learn that repeating shame's phrases kept shame alive, however, I vowed to stop. Can you see how repeating to yourself that you're worthless keeps that shame belief going? Healing those false shame-beliefs requires more than just stopping the negative self-talk, but it is an important first step. We'll explore this more in a later chapter.

Does our shame-speak consist of the actual words our caretakers said to us? Yes and no. Sometimes our caretakers did hurl these cruel, inaccurate messages at us, but many times, we developed these beliefs about ourselves as we tried to make sense of their lack of love or support, their rejection, or their meanness. We could only conclude it must be due to something defective in us. Why else would they withhold love, abuse us, or ignore us? Why else would they criticize us at every turn? As children, we don't have the perspective to see that our parents are troubled, emotionally untethered, or unloving. We didn't know our caretakers had their own shame-speak, and often those words they hurled at us were probably how they thought of themselves. We couldn't discern that these words were unfair, inaccurate, and cruel. In addition, our nervous system assessed that it was safer to submit–collapse–appease and blame ourselves because we could not survive if we were emotionally abandoned by our caretakers.

Understanding the role of projection

Taking the unacceptable traits and feelings we have about ourselves and accusing other people of having those qualities is called "projection." For example, a husband who lies to cover up a gambling problem accuses his wife of lying and hiding things from him; or a parent who wants to talk with her friends and look through Instagram accuses her children of being needy, and selfish.

How do we know when someone is projecting? When someone accuses us of something that is not true about us, we should be suspicious that it is projection. But as children, did we know what was true about us? No. Instead, we believed that our parents knew best. Even if we disagreed, we couldn't fight them or run away. Instead, we accepted their false messages about who we were and incorporated them into our inner dialogue regarding who we believed ourselves to be. That became part of our shame-speak.

As children, we also unconsciously surmised that if we could fix our defective little selves, our parents would love and appreciate us. In our attempts to win them over, we often adopted a stance of perfectionism and self-criticism, believing that if we could criticize ourselves into being who they wanted, they would love us. This was our best attempt to win the love and protection of our parental figures. We had no idea that their lack of loving us had little to do with us and was, instead, a terrible handicap that they had developed long before we arrived.

You aren't alone

We often believe that shame has a message just for us—one that others don't hear. We also imagine others are less damaged, less pathetic, and less messed up. But rest assured, the putdowns and negative judgments we hear in our own minds are the same for everyone. Shame takes our experiences of being emotionally rejected, ignored, betrayed, smothered, and abused, wraps them in our personal narratives, and labels them "especially true for you." Believing that others don't have these same thoughts and feelings, we feel alone in our brokenness. This is the poison of toxic shame. It keeps us believing that no one is as flawed as we are and no one will accept someone so broken, and so, we keep our pain to ourselves. We spend a lot of time and energy worried that if others could see our brokenness, they would reject us.

But we are not alone with our shame. There are thousands and thousands of us. As we learn to hear our shame-speak, we become more proficient at identifying shame-speak in others. Those others are the millions of folks who hurt from shame, just as we do.

As I got to know my neighbor, David, he shared a few stories about how critical and demeaning his father had been to him growing up. But I didn't fully realize the impact of his childhood shame until one day when he agreed to help me load a reel of new line into my weed eater. It had been fifteen years since I had added a new spool, and I couldn't remember how to do it. We stood together in my garage as he struggled to twist and pry open the housing. It was corroded and tricky to figure out, and after a few minutes, he said, "Well, this will certainly make you think less of me."

That's shame-speak for sure, I thought. I felt sad and said to him as warmly as I could, "David, of course, I'm not going to think less of you! Don't be silly. I couldn't figure it out either. It's nothing to be ashamed of." But my reassurance may not have done much to change his shame feelings. Still, I hoped he would think about it and that someday we could talk about shame.

Code words for shame

When we mindlessly repeat shame-speak's ugly phrases, we are working for shame. We are the ones who keep the wounds open. Therefore, an essential first step in healing our shame is to become aware of our shame-speak. This isn't easy because it is so familiar, but knowing the vocabulary helps us recognize it. Become proficient at recognizing your shame talk. Listen to what you say, listen to what you think, and don't allow yourself to habitually, mindlessly perpetuate your shame by accepting and repeating its phrases. This is the beginning of waking ourselves out of our hypnotic trance of shame beliefs.

Here are some common shame words. I feel … ridiculous, foolish, silly, idiotic, stupid, dumb, humiliated, disrespected, helpless, weak, inept, dependent, small, inferior, unworthy, worthless, trivial, despicable, shy, uncomfortable, or embarrassed. (Dearing and Tangney 2011)

Which of these phrases have you heard yourself saying to yourself?

- "I'm sorry to be such a bother. I'm sorry to be a nuisance. I'm sorry."
- "I'm so stupid—what an idiot."
- "I'm such a loser."
- "I'm too emotional. I cry for no reason."
- "I shouldn't feel that way."
- "I hate myself for asking too many questions."
- "Of course, I screwed it up. What do you expect? I'm a screw-up."
- "No one wants to help me. I'm such a bother."
- "I was born with a dark cloud over my head. Others can see it."
- "What's wrong with me?"
- "No one is going to love me when they find out my flaws."
- "I'm too broken."
- "I'm too fat, ugly, old, (you name it) to be lovable."

And when a child is shamed by smothering parents:

"I can't cope without my mother."
"I will be no one when my mother dies."
"My father always knows the right thing to do. He knows better than I do. I need him."

These are the words and phrases we apply to describe the feelings and sensations our shame triggers in us. Perhaps they're also things people said to us directly. But whatever the source, now we know that these self-deprecating phrases are symptoms of our wounds. They describe how broken we feel because of how we were treated. *They don't describe our real self.* When these words come into our minds, we mustn't let them go out of our mouths. This step alone will at least stop further damage.

As we wake up from our "trance of unworthiness" (Brach) and see what we're doing to ourselves, we can choose to be vigilant and stop it. We can't heal our wounds if we continue to drink the arsenic of these lies. Let's unpack the lies one by one in the next chapter and see the real truth behind them.

Replacing shame-speak with self-affirming and true statements about yourself is essential. Chapter 14, "The Wounding of False Mirroring and Projection," in Part 2 will walk you through a process to reject the shame-speak messages and create your own truth.

Chapter Takeaways

1. Shame is an insidious emotion that manifests in self-criticism and self-deprecating statements which we come to believe are true about ourselves.
2. Self-deprecating phrases such as "How stupid can you be?" or the frequent use of "I'm sorry" reflect the feelings of brokenness, unworthiness, and inadequacy that are characteristic of shame.
3. Repeating these self-deprecating phrases perpetuates shame. The words are not harmless. They are self-assaulting and corrosive.
4. The mind does not know the difference between what others say to us and what we say to ourselves. Think about how you may have focused on what others said and not given enough attention to stopping your own harsh words.
5. Many of the false accusations we hear as children are examples of projection, which is when parents or other authority figures accuse us of having traits and feelings they possess but reject as true about themselves.
6. Recognizing shame-speak is a crucial step in healing shame. By recognizing the vocabulary of shame and being mindful of the phrases we say to ourselves, we can stop our shame-speak.

Reflection Question

Reflecting on the self-deprecating statements you make to yourself, especially when you make a mistake or feel insecure, how do these statements keep your shame beliefs alive? Write in your notebook about your thoughts, insights, and how you'd like to change this habit.

Practice

1. Every time you hear yourself saying a self-deprecating statement, stop and notice it. Don't let it fly out of your mouth as though it was nothing.
2. Sometimes we don't even notice these phrases. Ask a friend whom you talk to regularly or a trusted person in your household to point them out to you. When I did this, I was surprised by how often I verbalized shame-speak and never even noticed it.
3. Write down in your notebook the shame-speak phrases you hear yourself say. Be on the lookout for when you say them without even thinking.

4

Unmasking Shame's Lies

Shame is a response to something that happened, and it needs the same kind of attention that sadness, for example, needs so that it doesn't become a chronic, draining feeling.

—Patricia DeYoung

A client recently told me she was in a situation where she was getting complimented for her accomplishments, but all she could hear in her head were the words, "Wait until they get to know you. They won't think so highly of you then."

"Did you believe that was true?" I asked her.

"Yes, I guess I did, because I've always believed that."

Then I suggested, "Maybe it was true in some circumstances, but it's probably a lot more complicated than people not liking you when they get to know you."

The words we hear in our minds (shame-speak) and the ways we feel about ourselves reflect the sense we tried to make of the way our primary caretakers treated us and what they projected onto us. Janina Fisher directly addresses why children accept the blame for how their parents treat them. Remember that Fisher wrote that children would rather accept the blame than believe their parents will not protect and love them.

We accepted these lies about ourselves as truth because we were children caught in a no-win cruel bind. But let's look at these beliefs from our adult perspective.

When people get to know me more, they won't like me.

Shame tells us to hide ourselves because we're not good enough, we're not acceptable. In fact, the word "shame" means to "veil oneself."

Remember the Still Face experiment and how the toddler was so frightened and then eventually collapsed when her mother wouldn't respond? This was a one-time situation, but what about those who experience an entire childhood of frightening experiences because of how they are raised? As children, we don't know why our parents neglect us, ignore us, hurt us physically, sexually abuse us, or threaten us. All we can do is try to hide the parts of ourselves that we think might have caused their mistreatment. We quickly learn to keep parts of ourselves hidden when we believe our caretakers will object to those parts, and we don't let our caretakers know our honest thoughts or feelings. We believe that revealing too much about ourselves—our needs, fears, anger, and retaliatory thoughts—would further alienate them from us. We try to mold ourselves into the child our parents want because we want them to love and protect us. This pattern continues into adulthood and infiltrates all our relationships, especially the ones we are most invested in. For example we often try to be who we think our romantic partners want, fearing they will otherwise reject us.

My needs are too much. I shouldn't be so needy.

Your needs may have been more than your caretakers could manage, but all children are needy. If your caretaker was depressed, emotionally compromised, overwhelmed, addicted, or rejecting, your needs might have been too much for *them*. This wasn't because you were too needy but because they couldn't adequately respond. Their messages about your needs were about their capacity, not about you. In another family, you would have received different messages about your needs. Besides, children have needs for everything. That's the very definition of childhood.

If you're getting messages as an adult that your needs are too much, here is something to consider. Maybe the person telling you this isn't prepared to respond to your level of need, not because they're bad or you're wrong but because everyone has limits. Their limits are a message about them, not about you.

For example, a client I know yearned for more emotional connection and conversation with her husband. When she pressed him, however, he routinely told her she was too needy and that all she wanted to talk about were problems. This frustrated and angered her, which led to fights and even less conversation. As she tried to understand her husband better, she remembered that he had always been a man of few words. He showed his caring by fixing things and making a good living. "He's a doer," she observed. "I'm a talker. I don't know how this will work out, but at least I'm not making him or myself wrong anymore."

"You're just too needy," a boyfriend told my client, Cynthia. Deeply hurt, yet caring about him, Cynthia wanted to talk about whether he might have a point. As I asked her to share some of the details, she explained that she often told him he didn't text her enough when he was at work. She also felt extra insecure when he was out of town on business and insisted on knowing who he was meeting. If it was a woman and he had drinks or dinner after the meeting, she panicked, texting and calling him until he responded. After hearing several more similar examples, I gently told her that I could see she felt insecure and wanted her boyfriend to comfort and reassure her. She agreed. I asked if she'd had similar feelings in previous relationships. "I always feel insecure and afraid once I get invested in a relationship."

"Well," I said. "I think you've made a good decision to talk with someone about this. You deserve to understand where those feelings come from and how to heal them. You and I can work on your fears and insecurities so that you and your boyfriend can work on creating fun."

"You mean it *is* me?" she asked.

"Chances are that many of your insecurities and fears began long before you met this man or any of your previous boyfriends. You have insecurities for a good reason, and a romantic relationship may help with insecurities, but it does not heal them. You will need to do much of the healing through your own self-acceptance. Then the caring of a boyfriend can add to that. A romantic relationship can *help* you heal, but the majority of your healing is an inside job and one I am sure you are very capable of doing."

My behavior defines who I am.

Your behavior has nothing to do with the core of who you are any more than a cloud defines the sky. Maybe as an older child, you were unruly or disobedient. Perhaps you stole or broke things or didn't do as you were told. But from your adult perspective, can you see that those behaviors were the normal and understandable actions of an angry or unhappy child? What makes children angry? Not being loved or treated fairly and never feeling good enough.

When I misunderstand or can't articulate what I think, it's because I am stupid.

We all misunderstand and get tongue-tied, especially when we feel anxious or threatened. If our brain is scanning for danger while we're trying to think, our brains go into overload, and the problem-solving function goes offline. When we feel anxious, painfully self-conscious, or threatened, our priority is safety, survival, and minimizing the threat. In these situations, our access to words is diminished. As our brain and nervous system assess the danger, our brain mutes down or shuts off our ability to think. It has nothing to do with intelligence. It has to do with feeling frightened and being in a survival response. Research confirms this.

Big emotions mean I'm mentally off. Normal people are logical and calm.

Ideally, as children, we learn how to regulate our intense emotions from the soothing and comfort our caretakers provide. For example, when we're young and our caretaker picks us up and talks softly to us, their calm body and soothing voice help us regulate our own nervous system. Unfortunately, as children, we can't do this for ourselves unless someone else has done it for us many times over a period of years. Therefore, many of us—me included— as adults must intentionally learn calming words to say to ourselves in stressful or frightening situations. I've learned that I feel better when I remember to tell myself: You're going to be okay. You're safe. You aren't alone. Everything is going to be fine. Breathe.

We'll explore more ways to comfort and soothe yourself later in the book, but for now, know this: If you struggle with wild emotions or dark moods, it may be because your care-taker didn't help you learn how to modulate your emotions. It isn't because something is broken in you or wrong with you.

Asking questions is a nuisance. I should be seen and not heard.

Sadly in many troubled families, questions are just a form of talking back, sassing, and showing disrespect. Children are naturally curious as they try to figure things out. Asking questions is part of being a child. For example, "Why did you say no?" is a question asking for informa-tion. So is, "Mommy, why are you so angry?" But that isn't how shame-generating caretakers see it. To them, questions threaten their authority and control. "You'll do it because I told you to!" is something overwhelmed and authoritarian parents often say to children.

Children also have a keen sense of fairness, so when something seems unfair, they naturally question it—unless they've been shamed into submission. Contrary to the mes-sages you may have received, your curiosity is a gift. It means you are bright and engaged and you want information.

Some people deserve things, and others don't. Therefore, I shouldn't aspire to things I don't deserve.

Overwhelmed and overextended parents often use the concept of "deserving" to explain why they can't meet their children's needs. For example, if your family is struggling financially, you may have been told you didn't deserve things because your parents couldn't provide them. Rather than saying, "I wish I could buy you that Halloween costume because I see how much you like it," they might say, "Don't be so selfish. You know we can't afford things like that." One of my clients told me that her parents would routinely ask her, "Do you deserve it?" whenever she asked for things. What kind of a question is that? It's a statement designed to make the child feel bad and to hide the parents' inadequacy.

Mistakes always indicate some defect. There are no accidents, and someone is always to blame.

Often, we are scolded or humiliated for making mistakes, as though feeling horrible about yourself will eliminate mistakes. However, mistakes happen to everyone and can be valuable learning opportunities. Consider this: Thomas Edison apparently had 1,500 failed experiments before he discovered the secret to electricity. What if he had been shamed out of making mistakes? The message that mistakes are bad and someone is to blame just isn't true. Mistakes are the way we learn.

People don't care enough about me to go out of their way for me.

If your caretakers weren't available to support and protect you when you needed them, your young mind assumed something about you was the cause. In some families, asking for help can be dangerous. One client told me she frequently heard, "Can't you see I'm busy? I don't have time for every little thing you think you need. I'm not here to serve you. Do it yourself." Another client told me her mother would say,

"Your problem is not my issue. You figure it out." Many parents who say these cruel and rejecting things are themselves struggling and their attitudes toward us have nothing to do with us. But these messages hurt us, and the belief that we aren't worthy of care lingers until we heal the parts of us that carry those beliefs.

I'm just unlucky, and that's how it is for some people.

Luck, they say, is what happens when preparation meets opportunity. When we're focused on surviving the emotional landmines in our family, we don't have much energy left over to create opportunities. In addition, dysfunctional families often don't create the same opportunities for their children that more functional families do. Also, chances are that your parents attributed their own lack of success to bad luck or to someone being a jerk.

My client, Amy, told me that she wanted to try out for cheerleading in high school. Her parents, however, thought it would take up too much time that should be spent helping around the house. Her father got angry when he caught her practicing cheers in their yard. Since she'd had little practice when she tried out for the cheerleading team, she fell during one of the routines and wasn't chosen.

Her conclusion at that time was that she was just unlucky. But as she got older, she saw others succeeding in what interested them and became curious about how they did it. "One girl in high school always got all As, and when I jokingly asked her how she did it, she told me how many hours a day she studied. I was amazed. That was twice as many as I studied. I think that's when I realized that if you want things to happen in your life, you must put in the preparation. It's not about luck."

I'm nothing without my parents.

Our parents are important in many ways, but as adolescents and adults, we grow by learning to trust our own judgment and weathering the inevitable storms that come our way. It's our right, in fact, to develop and practice skills and grow confidence in our own abilities. Sadly, when our parents' caring is overdone, it's much like over-watering a house plant. It won't thrive and grow into a healthy, sturdy, beautiful plant, and neither can we. Love never involves "over-watering" or creating dependency.

I'm unique in how broken I am.

You're definitely unique, but your "brokenness" has nothing to do with your uniqueness. One thing I learned in my profession is how common it is to feel broken. When our parents don't sufficiently love us, we think it's because of some defect in us. But it's far more likely that they just didn't know how to love us. It had nothing to do with us. Think about it. Can you see that your parent or caretaker didn't know how to love unconditionally, even though it's something that children need and deserve? Our mental-emotional well-being depends on having a reliable, steady, loving person to catch us when we fall and love us through the storms.

Shame-speak is so insidious and familiar that unless we're vigilant and determined to monitor and challenge the messages, the words will continue to be our beliefs about ourselves. Then our actions will reflect how we feel about ourselves. Our choice of friends, career decisions, goals, and how we treat our romantic partners and children is affected by what we believe is true about us. But we can choose to heal ourselves! And we can begin by stopping ourselves from repeating shame-phrases and from passively believing shame's messages. This is how we begin to heal our shame.

As you continue to heal, the belief "my mother will love me *if* I'm good enough" will give way to "my mother may never love me, and I'm still lovable." The belief "I'm broken and can never be whole" will recede, and you will come to know "I'm whole and lovable, and I always have been so."

———

Chapter Takeaways

1. Children who experience repeated shame blame themselves for the harm inflicted upon them by others—"hating themselves when they could not risk hating those who hurt them."
2. Our shame-based thoughts and feelings originate from the way primary caregivers treated us and the projection of their own issues.
3. We have many misbeliefs about ourselves stemming from our parents' immaturity and inadequacy. We can learn the truth about these misbeliefs and change them.

Reflection Question

How do you feel about asking for help? Do you hesitate and worry that the other person will find your request bothersome or irritating?

Practice

Notebook in hand:
1. What are three of your most prevalent shame-based beliefs about yourself?
2. What would you like to believe about yourself instead? For example, you might say, "When I forget what I'm saying or can't recall a fact I need to make my point, it's NOT because I'm not smart. Being anxious or under pressure causes people's cognitive abilities to go offline or slow down. I'm nervous, not stupid!"

5

Not All Shame Looks the Same

Shame hurts. If our shame is exposed, it can be unbearable. To save ourselves, we push shame away as fast as we can, covering it with more tolerable states of being.

—Patricia DeYoung

We may think a politician's aggressive, demeaning rhetoric has no similarity to the shy, reclusive woman down the street, but it does. At their core, both are dealing with deep toxic shame. One strategy puffs up and attacks, while the other deflates and hides.

Shame is disguised under behavior we would not think of as shame. If we only think shame is evidenced by downcast eyes, shy behavior, and a slumped posture, we are missing the fact that shame is often covered over by aggression and a hyperdrive for success and recognition. But these disguises are "compensations and collapses, masks, slights of mind; they are not shame itself … but a camouflage," wrote Patricia DeYoung. (DeYoung 2015). By understanding the disguises shame hides behind, we see how epidemic shame really is.

In 1992, psychiatrist Donald Nathanson, a significant contributor to the study of shame, identified four shame disguises. In his book, *Shame and Pride* (Nathanson 1992), he referred to them as the "compass of shame," depicting them as the four directions of a compass. Nathanson labeled the shame-driven behaviors as *attack self, attack others, withdraw, and avoid feeling.* These responses are linked to survival strategies. For example, when a shame-prone child (someone who has habitually responded with *collapse–submit–appease*) gets older, maybe around adolescence, their nervous system and brain may choose *fight* and *attack others* instead of the shame response. In this way, the outside world views them as tough and aggressive rather than ashamed and collapsed. It's a powerful, clever, and effective survival strategy.

Do we pick our shame disguises the way we'd pick a Halloween outfit? Not really. But by late childhood or adolescence, we begin to assemble a repertoire of disguises that throw others off any scent of shame and help shield us from further shame. By trial and error, we learn what works and what doesn't, and we also look to see what our significant caretaker has modeled.

Not only do these shame disguises fool others, but many shamed people don't recognize their behavior as a shame disguise. They do not realize that their self-attacks or aggressive behaviors are hidden shame. Even if they wanted to understand their behavior, it would be challenging without the awareness that shame was driving that behavior.

As you read through the following descriptions of the four points of the compass of shame, remember that these ways of operating in the world are a person's attempts to hide how worthless and *not good enough* they feel. Their minds craft a way to hide their woundedness. While each description is distinct, most people use a combination, depending on their history and the circumstances.

Attack-self strategy—the appease–submit–collapse survival response

This is the pattern we generally associate with shame. We can recognize it in ourselves by observing the shame-speak we hear in our minds or say to ourselves. It will be critical and demeaning. Our bodies also show the years of beating ourselves up. Our posture is likely slumped, our shoulders folded in, and our chest collapsed. If you step back and look at that posture, you can see that it is the stance of someone who feels defeated and wants to be as non-threatening as possible.

Self-deprecating shame-speak reinforces this collapsed orientation. This attack-self strategy creates a never-ending accumulation of self-inflicted wounding by believing other people are better, more successful, brighter, and more attractive. Our shame quickens as we compare ourselves to them and find ourselves lacking. We criticize ourselves with labels like stupid, selfish, thoughtless, too emotional, clumsy, too sensitive, and defective. Over time, attack-self thoughts become so dominant that they eat away at our fledgling self-esteem like "cannibalism in the mind," as an unknown author wrote; or, as Carl Jung said, "shame is a soul-eating emotion."

Attack-self scripts are common for kids raised by parents who used *attack others* as a method of child-rearing. These children feel helpless against the onslaught of criticism and the negation of their feelings. They accept that they're to blame for their parents' demeaning behavior and, sadly, these children often feel responsible for their abuse and mistreatment. By taking responsibility for their mistreatment, the child unconsciously believes that the injustice will stop if they can fix themselves. However, because they aren't the real source of their parents' difficulties, they can't change their parents, and their parents' mistreatment continues.

Self-attack is also a strategy that turns the anger and pain of being attacked inward toward the self. It's no wonder that attack-self behaviors can take the form of severe depression, eating disorders, anxiety, obsessive worry, self-mutilation (as in cutting and burning), and even suicide.

Attack others—the "fight" survival strategy

Attack others is a powerful strategy. As the fight hormone adrenaline pumps through the body, it empowers and emboldens the person. What more could a shamed self want? It feels so good to feel physically strong, sure of oneself, focused, unwavering, and righteous.

Furthermore, putting the other person on the defensive is remarkably effective. When the other person is thrown off balance, the attacker isn't suspected of feeling inferior or unworthy. By verbally or physically lashing out and attacking others—even if the attacker is at fault—the attention shifts away from the shame-filled attacking person toward the frightened, confused other person.

My stepfather was an expert at attacking others, especially when he was at fault. In my early twenties, he dropped me off at the Seattle airport for my return to college after a short visit. Pulling up to the curb, he carelessly swiped the car's fender behind him. Jumping out of the car, he started yelling, "Don't you know how to park, you idiot?! Meathead! How stupid can you be!" He grabbed my suitcase from the backseat, tossed it onto the sidewalk, and sped away—no warm goodbyes.

Intense anger is a sign of immense, unconscious shame. This isn't a wave of ordinary anger, but rather, a rage that seeks to *destroy* or *diminish* the other person. This kind of anger is at the root of domestic violence, schoolyard fighting, sarcastic putdowns, ridicule, contempt, public humiliation, and, at its most extreme, murder.

Withdrawal strategy—the "flight or flee" survival response

Consider Deborah, who was sixty-two when she consulted me because of debilitating depression. She always arrived late and frequently was wearing her bathrobe and slippers. During one session, she shared an incident about being shamed and bullied in middle school. Two of her male classmates falsely told other boys they'd had sex with her. Nothing could have been further from the truth. Deborah was shy and quiet as an adolescent. Although devastated by the accusations, she didn't confide in her mother, assuming that she would believe the allegations and blame her. Then, in a terrible twist, she was befriended by a neighbor boy who was also a classmate. Thinking he was her friend, she listened to his tales of what he alleged he had heard the children at school saying about her. Sadly, young Deborah believed him, and her shame grew deeper. She began avoiding other kids and missing school. When her mother uncharacteristically hosted a birthday party for her, none of her classmates showed up. Not one.

Deborah's adult years were focused on her career; otherwise, she was socially isolated. Her only acquaintances outside work were her paid help—a manicurist, hairdresser, gardener, and housekeeper. Her world grew even smaller when she retired and moved to a new town. She seldom left her house.

Withdrawal is the feeling of wanting to get away, crawl into a hole, and disappear. Triggered from the outside by others' behavior or internally by our own thoughts, it is the strategy of finding safety by staying physically and emotionally removed from others. In its more extreme state, it causes people to live a reclusive life devoid of close friends or intimate relationships. When the pain of not belonging is too great to bear, they act as though they don't care about belonging.

When we find ourselves disappearing from our lives— Brené Brown calls it going "offline": not returning calls and lying about what has caused our "disappearance"— we should suspect that we are having a shame attack. We might say, "I lost my phone," "I was sick," or "I lost track of time." Many times, we don't know what's happening. We only know that we feel too raw or deflated to venture out. It feels like withdrawing from a harsh and cruel world is the best strategy.

Avoidance strategy—a combination of survival responses

What Nathanson calls avoidance is a strategy of unconsciously *avoiding* any feeling or recognition of shame. When shame has been so devastatingly painful, we want to avoid even the possibility of "not good enough" feelings breaking into our awareness. Instead of raw shame, we may sense an uncomfortable feeling or an emotional wince inside. In social situations, we may squirm or exit the situation quickly, but we wouldn't label it as shame.

The *avoidance* strategy also uses many of the other strategies. Often seen as ruthless and self-focused, avoiders are in defensive mode, often shielding themselves by being cruel and demeaning to others. If the attention of others can be shifted to the demeaned, then being seen as inferior or damaged can be avoided. Consumed by attempts to keep any appearance of inferiority or weakness from being seen, avoiders adopt the motto, "whatever it takes."

Admitting wrongdoing is never acceptable. They won't make apologies, and confrontation won't be tolerated. When questioned, corrected, or criticized, the shamed avoider goes into a rage that is meant to destroy. They choose adoring and useful friends to compensate for their unconscious inferiority feelings about themselves. And to seal the deal, weakness or powerlessness in others is ridiculed and judged because it's just too close to home.

If the shame-pain does break through, misuse of drugs or medication often helps to temporarily relieve the painful feelings. So is staying obsessively busy. Avoiders are people with exaggerated drives to achieve—workaholics with excessive competitiveness and an obsession with looks, wealth, and sexual conquests. Any incompetence or imperfection is vehemently denied and blamed on someone else. Constantly comparing themselves to others, they're often boastful braggarts and bullies. We may think of them as narcissistic.

My client, Linda, was obsessed with exercise. Gaunt and frail, she was a successful scientist in the defense industry. But she was so obsessed with exercise that she was often late for work. She knew her boss was upset with her tardiness, and she was concerned she would get written up—something that would be humiliating.

Once a beautiful woman who prided herself on her career accomplishments and trim good looks, she was beginning to avoid social contact because of how she looked. Her body had started to show the stress of over-exercising. The final straw came when she attempted to lure a handsome man into having a nightcap at her house and he declined. That was when she called me.

Her exercise obsession began, she told me, when she discovered in high school how good running cross-country felt. She had joined the track team with the encouragement of a school counselor who recognized how depressed she was. When the endorphins kicked in, Linda said she felt the way she imagined others felt all the time.

As an adult, she chased that feeling, and who could blame her, except that it ruled her life. She spent all her free time exercising. She was skinny, tense, and lonely. As I got to know Linda more, she slowly and painfully talked about the humiliation and criticism she had received from her mother. Linda was never pretty, thin, or clever enough in her mother's eyes. Her early life shame had become disguised as depression with a thick blanket of unworthiness. But she didn't know it was shame; all she knew was that she had to keep exercising.

Recognizing disguises

As we ask ourselves whether we recognize these patterns in our own behaviors, remember that these are survival strategies—a young person's best attempts at protecting themselves from the pain of shame. These interpersonal styles created in childhood are perfected in early adulthood and become habitual and unconscious, taking over our behavior. In the past, we needed them, but as adults, we're operating on autopilot.

Research shows that these scripts appear to follow gender. Women are more likely to *attack-self* and *withdraw*. Perhaps they saw their mother drop her head in shame and call herself stupid when she misplaced her grocery list or lost the car keys. Men are more likely to use *attack-other* and *avoid feeling*. Attacking and blaming someone is more manly, and boys are socialized to fight rather than collapse. For boys and men, feeling the weakness of shame can be intolerable and sets them up for humiliating teasing and belittling. Gender aside, however, most people use a combination of these responses.

Choosing differently

As we learn to see beneath our shame disguises, we can sense the price we are paying for them. Part of our healing is identifying our patterns and then consciously choosing a different response. For example, when we see ourselves primed to attack someone because we feel embarrassed, threatened, belittled, or upset, we stop ourselves. In this way, we can begin to unravel this ingrained response habit. It's no small feat when we interrupt our old shame pattern of attacking others.

Likewise, if we're in the habit of withdrawing and staying to ourselves, we can encourage and reward ourselves for accepting an invitation to a work friend's party. These aren't trivial, but rather, monumental first steps. They are triumphs, and eventually, they'll aid in our emancipation from shame's grip.

Changing these patterns requires becoming aware of our behavior and deciding that these unhealthy and shame-driven ways aren't how we want to act. Healing our shame wounds will help shift these patterns, but even then, we need to intentionally decide that certain behaviors are no longer acceptable and consciously stop them. Why not begin now?

Do we still need these shame disguises? After all, they were formed to protect us. As I often tell my clients, the worst shaming you will ever experience likely happened in your past, when you were most vulnerable and dependent upon your caretakers. Hopefully, your current circumstances are kinder, and you don't need the protection you did in the past; if you do, it's always available.

By recognizing that shame can appear in many different outfits, we can be aware of our own shame disguises and those of others. Maybe we'll come to understand that our attacking caretaker was a person also driven by shame. Shame has afflicted thousands and thousands of people who may show it very differently than we do—but we all have been deeply hurt, and we deserve the opportunity to heal those wounds. We must begin the healing process by recognizing our patterns and choosing differently.

Chapter Takeaways

1. Shame is not always seen as shyness or a slumped posture. Sometimes shame disguises itself behind aggression, success-driven behaviors, withdrawal, or avoidance.
2. Shame disguises serve as survival strategies that we develop to protect ourselves from the pain of feeling worthless or not good enough.
3. The compass of shame: attack self, attack others, withdraw, and avoid feeling are survival strategy responses.
4. Many people who use shame disguises are unaware that their behaviors are rooted in shame. They may not recognize that their self-attacks or aggression toward others are ways of coping with their underlying shame.
5. Recognizing our shame disguises is a step in the process of healing from shame. But these disguises must be acknowledged before we can decide to actively change them. They don't change on their own.

Reflection Question

Reflecting on the four shame expressions and disguises, what are your mother's and your father's shame disguises? They may have combinations of patterns.

Practice

Notebook at the ready:

1. Do you recognize your shame disguises in the description of common shame disguises? Write them down.
2. Given your primary shame disguise, what behaviors could you do differently that would allow you to make a conscious choice that's different from your usual behavior? An example: If you recognize yourself as someone who attacks others by gossiping about them, you could decide to stop yourself when, historically, you would have said all kinds of things.

6

Shame's Toll on Empathy

Shame is an acutely painful emotion that can really interfere with empathic connection in close relationships.

—June Tangney

As I walked into my waiting room to meet my new client, Annette, I saw her four-year-old son staring at me, frozen in terror. An overturned vase of artificial flowers lay on the floor. "Look at what you've done!" Annette said in a cold reprimanding tone. "The lady's going to be so mad at you!" I was astonished by what she was saying to this frightened little guy. There wasn't an ounce of compassion in her voice. She had offered her little guy no comfort, understanding, or normalizing.

"Kids knock things over. It's okay. I'm not upset," I said, inviting them into my office.

Annette sat on a small sofa, and her little boy scrunched beside her. When I asked how I could help her, she told me she was worried about her two other sons. Both of them were doing poorly in school. Her oldest boy struggled with "reading and paying attention," and both boys were "shy and had no friends." She wondered aloud what was wrong with them and asked if I thought her older boys needed to see a counselor.

As we talked, I asked her to describe what it was like for her growing up in her family. She answered without elaborating that her childhood was "okay." Further inquiry revealed that Annette was the youngest of five children, and her mother was "really nice but really busy." When I asked about her father, she replied matter-of-factly, "He was okay, but he got mad a lot. So I stayed in my room, reading."

"Did staying in your room away from your siblings and parents seem unusual?" I asked her.

"No, I was the family bookworm."

As I thought about Annette's older sons' school troubles and lack of self-confidence, I also reflected on the surprising lack of empathy I witnessed toward her four-year-old. What in her own family experiences might be shaping how she parented? Was she raised with that kind of harshness? I didn't know, of course, but I did know that parents draw their parenting practices from how they were parented. Was she unwittingly repeating the parenting style that had kept her alone in her room reading?

Where is the empathy?

What do we mean by empathy? When someone feels sad, and we feel their sadness, that's empathy. The *American Heritage Dictionary* defines empathy as "the ability to identify with or understand the perspective, experiences, or motivations of another individual and to comprehend and share another individual's emotional state." Empathy allows us to tune into another person's inner world by picking up on facial expressions, tone of voice, gestures, and even small heart rate and breathing changes. When we're empathetic and in sync with another person, we have a visceral, not intellectual, sense of what the other person is feeling.

When someone extends empathy to us, we feel seen and understood. "Knowing that we are seen and heard by the important people in our lives makes us feel calm and safe." (Van der Kolk 2014) An attentive, empathic connection, whether with a child or an adult, can shift us from feeling upset, scattered, and fearful to enjoying a steady, reassured, and calm state. It's a beautiful feeling—a true gift.

Some people are aware that they have difficulty with empathy. One evening, a dear friend sheepishly told me how ashamed she felt about her inability to feel other peoples' feelings. "When my friends talk to me about their feelings, even when they tell me about their mother dying or their brother getting pancreatic cancer, I listen to them, and I can see how distressed they are, but I don't *feel* how they feel. Instead, I try to imagine how someone in their situation might feel, and then I try to say something I think would be caring and kind. I see other people whose empathy just rolls out of them, and I want to be like that, too. But instead, I have to think my way through it. It makes me wonder what's wrong with me."

I knew just how she felt. This was my secret struggle too. My friend and I were both raised in shame-generating families, and as I told her I understood her struggle, we agreed it felt reassuring to know we weren't the only ones. However, it didn't help us feel any better about ourselves and certainly didn't change our damaged empathy.

For many years, I continued to be aware of how my empathy gene seemed to be missing, and I often asked myself, "What's wrong with me?"

Research shows that those who are shame-prone because they grew up in a shaming family *are low on empathy*. (Tangney and Dearing 2002) This statement may seem harsh, but as we will see, children who were shamed either intentionally or unintentionally develop critical strategies that protect them emotionally as children. Unfortunately, these unconscious strategies that help protect kids from being emotionally overwhelmed also diminish or block the development of empathy.

Children are naturally inclined to be empathic

Contrary to some common beliefs, children are naturally inclined to be empathetic. In one study spanning twelve weeks, twenty-one preschoolers from four to five years old were observed and interviewed (by an experimenter with whom they were familiar) about their spontaneous behaviors of helping, sharing, or comforting peers. As researchers, Eisenberg-Berg and Neal wrote, "When the examiner asked the children about their actions, the kids attributed their helpful behaviors by referring to the other's needs and pragmatic considerations." (Eisenberg-Berg and Neal 1979) These behaviors included helping another student who was struggling to put on his coat or sharing a snack with someone who didn't have one. None of the children said they did this because they feared being punished or reprimanded. There was no difference by gender or age.

Empathic responses are measured in brain activity

In a 2008 study using MRI scans, Jean Decety, Professor in the Departments of Psychology and Psychiatry at the University of Chicago, found that seven- to twelve-year-old children showed a measurable neural (brain wave) response to both seeing others in pain and seeing someone cause pain to someone else. "The programming for empathy is something that is 'hard-wired' into the brains of normal (typically developing) children, and not entirely the product of parental guidance or other nurturing," Decety wrote. (Decety 2010) Some children understand it without much effort, while others need more practice.

If we're naturally empathic and attuned to others' feelings and needs, how can adults and parents end up with inhibited empathy? What causes the shame-prone to be less empathic than others raised in loving and supportive families? My experience and the experiences of my clients suggest that a theory proposed by Nathanson is worth exploring.

Empathic barriers

Psychiatrist and professor Donald Nathanson, MD, was one of the first to identify the lack of empathy in his shame-prone patients. He suggested that they suffered from what he called an "empathic barrier." (Nathanson 1992) As he searched for a possible cause, he noted that these patients had grown up in families in which at least one caretaker was emotionally distressed or emotionally unhealthy. Sometimes it was an excessively angry parent or depressed mother.

Sometimes the primary parent was clinging and overprotec-
tive or fearful and anxious about their child's safety and their
own well-being. A few parents were mentally ill. From these
observations, Nathanson suggested that the children unconsciously protected themselves from feeling the caretakers'
emotional misery because it was a burden they couldn't bear.
They had to create an "empathic barrier" to save themselves.

On the surface, feeling another's feelings seems like a
good thing. But the pain of having a wide-open child's heart
can be too much when, for example, a mother's sadness
and hopelessness add a terrible weight to the child's own
emotional heaviness. Not only is their mother emotionally
unavailable to them, which is the shame of what's missing,
but the child also absorbs her distress. Likewise, a lonely
father who feels estranged from his wife and leans on a child
for physical or emotional closeness can feel like a responsibility the child can't bear.

Sometimes, overwhelming pain in a family comes from
watching the mistreatment of siblings or their unfair and
harsh punishment.

I felt some relief when I learned about the "empathic
barrier" theory. With this explanation, I understood that my
friend and I had walled off our hearts for the sake of survival. I had a way of understanding my deficit, and while I
regretted the handicap, I didn't feel ashamed of it anymore.
Instead, I felt like I wasn't damaged but wounded and that I
would find a way to open my heart again.

Another explanation for the difficulty that shame-prone
people experience in being empathetic comes from the work
of Tangney and Dearing. Shame, as many have written, is

an emotion that causes us to be self-focused. It is the only emotion that causes us to look at ourselves and find ourselves lacking. Because we believe what shame tells us, we are worried that others will see our defects, and we are painfully self-scrutinizing. "But this tremendous preoccupation with the self draws one's focus away from the distressed other person, thus short-circuiting other-oriented feelings of empathy." (Tangney and Dearing 2002) In other words, shamed individuals are less likely concerned with the pain or feelings of the other, and are consumed with a focus on their own negative characteristics; meanwhile, the shame-speak is relentless: "I am such a loser. They'll probably hate me now. How could I be so pathetically stupid!"

I believe both theories have merit. Both theories definitely capture my experiences.

Parents' lack of empathy

As you look back on your early life, did you ever ask yourself if your parents could *feel* that their behavior and harsh words were hurting you and perhaps your siblings? Could they feel their children's pain? Did they look into their child's eyes and think, "I've got to stop—this isn't right!"? Sadly, the answer too often is "no." Your parents may have lacked genuine empathy, perhaps due to being raised in their own shame-generating family or situation. This is the terrible cost of generational shame; it fosters a detachment from the pain or feelings of others, including our own children, spouses, and loved ones. This is one of many reasons that shame-generating parenting must stop.

When we can't feel empathy

I watched an enthusiastic aunt play peekaboo with her baby nephew one afternoon. After a bit, the baby began signaling to the aunt that he wanted a break from their play. As the baby turned away and began disengaging, the aunt ramped up her energy and continued the game. When the baby started to fuss, the aunt responded, "What, you don't like your auntie?" Misreading the baby's messages, she persisted until the baby pushed her hands away and began to cry. This family member was unaware of what was happening and concluded the child just wanted his mother. Because she wasn't empathically attuned to her nephew, she didn't register that *her* invasive and insensitive reaction to his signals was responsible for his distress. An empathic barrier, or our self-focused self-concern, makes us oblivious to how our behavior can be empathically deficient even in the most casual interactions.

A relative of mine, in his sixties, told me about attending a family reunion where he encountered a young girl he didn't recognize.

"Whose kid are you?" he asked her.

Proudly, she replied, "I'm Wendy, Jack's youngest daughter."

"Oh," my relative remarked, "you're that bratty kid I met a few years ago."

I was flabbergasted and angry when he told me this, but when I expressed my reaction, he countered with, "Oh, I was just teasing." Having grown up in a family where cruel putdowns were considered funny, he didn't see the harm. I doubt he connected his derisive humor with how painful it was for him when he was the target of derogatory teasing. I believe he meant no harm and couldn't *feel* how humiliating his words were to that little girl. Still, that's *no excuse.*

If we have shielded ourselves from disturbing emotions by unconsciously creating an empathic barrier, empathy doesn't just magically develop when we reach adulthood. Why would we want more empathy? When we consider that empathy is a glue that leads to happier relationships in all areas of our lives, we can imagine how it can benefit us at work, with our spouses and children, in our communities, and as global citizens. Consciously working to dissolve your empathic barrier and reclaim this natural ability is *essential* for healthy interpersonal relationships.

Empathy is a form of curiosity: curiosity about what others are feeling. As children in hostile or emotionally burdensome environments, we may have shut down that curiosity or focused it on our pets, our fantasy games, or anything that shielded us from humans.

The following are some ideas about how to reconnect with and build empathy:

1. Become curious about people you don't know. Empathetic people are curious about those around them. They go beyond "What do you think of this weather?" and ask questions that allow them to get a glimpse into others' lives unobtrusively. "What's it like to have a small baby?" we might ask the woman in front of us in line. "Does your baby sleep through the night?" Listen. Let them tell you what it's like to be them.

2. Much of being empathic involves paying attention. Put your device away, make eye contact, and listen.

Notice facial expressions and gestures. Stop any thoughts of judging or prejudice, or the common habit of thinking about a comparable situation in your life that you want to share. Your mind should be empty except to attend to the person you are with.

3. Empathy involves two parts of the brain. The emotional part perceives another's feelings, and the cognitive center tries to understand why they feel as they do. You may never feel as they do in an analogous situation, which is why we tend to judge. But this is not about the right or wrong way to feel. It's not about how they got into this situation and whether you think it was poor judgment. This is about extending compassion and unbiased understanding to another human being.

4. Another way to strengthen our ability to perceive and attend to another's emotional world is to watch a movie or TV series and ask yourself, "What are they feeling?" A study conducted by Paul Zak (a neuroeconomist who studies human decision-making) and William Casebeer (a neurobiologist who studies how stories affect the human brain) showed that watching a compelling narrative can alter brain chemistry. When the study's participants watched a film about a father raising a son with terminal cancer, their brains created two neurochemicals: cortisol and oxytocin. Cortisol focuses attention by triggering a sense of distress, while oxytocin generates empathy by triggering our sense of care. Oxytocin is a chemical that gives a sense of

well-being to the person experiencing it. Perhaps the participants related to the film's characters. We know that empathy for someone familiar or with whom we identify is easier than for someone we perceive as different from ourselves. But Coan also says empathy is like a muscle, and "the more you use it, the stronger it becomes."

A study published in the *Journal of Applied Social Psychology* in 2014 found that watching movies and reading books can also generate empathy for people we perceive as very different from ourselves. After reading Harry Potter books, participants of the study showed greater empathetic responses to people in LGBT communities, immigrants, and other definable "outgroups." The researchers concluded that engaging with Harry Potter's story—filled with characters working to overcome prejudices and searching for how to fit in—helped participants better understand other people's perspectives. As Roger Ebert, the great film critic, said, "The movies are like a machine that generates empathy." (Finke 2015)

You were born curious about other people. Become curious again and recognize any barriers you have to forming empathic connections. Remember that empathy is like a muscle, and as you practice, you'll get better at it. I can assure you that empathy is at the top of emotional intelligence. You will reap more friends, happiness, and even success as you get better at it.

Chapter Takeaways

1. Empathy is defined as the ability to understand and feel another person's emotional state. Empathy goes beyond intellectual understanding to a visceral felt experience of their emotions.
2. Research indicates that individuals who grew up in shaming families tend to have lower levels of empathy. But all children are born with a natural capacity for empathy; therefore, you were too.
3. There are two theories about blunted empathy: a) Shame causes us to focus inward on our per-ceived flaws, and because we are so self-focused, it is challenging to connect with and understand others' emotions. b) An "empathic barrier" is when individ-uals protect themselves from emotional distress by unconsciously shutting down their ability to feel and understand the emotions of others.
4. Blunted empathy, whatever the cause, may persist into adulthood. But it can be understood and dismantled.

Reflection Question

Facing our empathy limitations can be difficult. Understanding why we may have muted down our empathy from an early age can be reassuring. What have you noticed about your ability to empathically connect to others?

Practice

1. Next time you listen to your friend or family member discuss something important to them, focus on your heart (not your judging thoughts about them or thoughts about yourself).
2. Ask yourself these questions: *How must that person be feeling? What do their eyes tell me? What do their facial expressions or body posture show me?*
3. Write in your notebook what you noticed about your ability to stay tuned in and to feel a bit of what they were expressing.
4. Did your mind want to judge?
5. Did your mind race to a comparable situation you'd experienced? Empathy is about staying focused on the other and not becoming engrossed in a memory or story from your own experiences.

7

Shame's Legacy in Parenting Practices

We learned shame in our earliest, most influential educational institution. We call it the family.

—Sandra Wilson

When I was about ten, I was visiting my grandmother and saw a neighbor boy hiding in the bushes. When I finally got a good view of him, I could see that his parents had shaved his head and were forcing him to wear his sister's dress. Even at ten, I knew this punishment was cruel. But, unfortunately, the intentional use of shame to punish has a long and miserable history.

How did harsh and shaming practices become so common in our culture? Why is this important to know? Because many of the parenting practices we were raised with came from emotionally unhealthy beliefs and advice. These practices began long before people understood the importance of raising emotionally healthy and resilient children. Instead, many age-old parenting practices focused on obedience and control by using fear, intimidation, and physical punishment. We now know this kind of parenting sets off survival alarms, and when used repeatedly, they're the source of toxic shame and all kinds of emotional issues. But we did not know that until fairly recently in human history.

In the 1950s, mental health experts began to gather science-based evidence that a child's emotional needs are as important as their physical needs. (It was also around this time that adults were seen as having emotional needs as well.) However, this information didn't put a stop to centuries-old, emotionally traumatizing parenting practices such as ignoring a crying child or harshly pushing away a clinging toddler, verbal threats, hitting, isolation, or ignoring a child for prolonged periods. How was it that we ever thought such emotionally painful treatment could be a good parenting practice?

The history of parenting advice

As I was tracing the origins of shame-generating parenting models, I remembered author Alice Miller (1923–2010), a German psychiatrist, whose work I had read years earlier. Her research stuck in my mind because she had used the phrase "soul murder" to describe the devastating effects of harsh and abusive parenting practices, especially emotional abuse. When I first read her work, I didn't label soul murder as shame-based parenting, but I certainly would now.

In *For Your Own Good: Hidden Cruelty in Child-Rearing and the Roots of Violence* (Miller 1990), Miller goes back to the mid-1800s and explains the influence of Moritz Schreber, a well-known and respected German physician, child psychiatrist, and professor. Schreber's parenting advice is shockingly harsh, even abusive by today's standards. But it was widely read in Europe and America, with forty print-ings between 1850 and 1860. His underlying philosophy reflected many of the beliefs of his time—children are born with dangerous and corrupting traits, and the parent must correct and eliminate them. Some attributed these traits to original sin, but whatever the origins, Schreber advocated early interventions beginning in infancy.

According to Schreber, a parent's goal was "unwavering obedience." A child's crying or screaming was "the first test of a parent's adherence to spiritual and child-raising prin-ciples," he wrote, "and warned that a child expressing their needs is an act of willfulness." He advised that this terrible trait should be met with stern words, threatening gestures such as rapping on the bed, and, as a last resort, "appropri-ate mild corporal admonishments" (physical hitting). After a few repetitions of such child-rearing practices, Schreber promised that a mere glance or threatening words would control the child.

Parenting advice in America

Eight decades after Schreber, John Watson's best-selling par-enting advice was published in *The Psychological Care of the Infant and Child* (Watson 1928). A renowned American psy-chologist, Watson (1878–1958) founded the psychological school of Behaviorism. Unlike Freud and Jung's psycholo-gies, Behaviorism focuses on shaping behavior—feelings, inner thoughts, or the subconscious are not the focus. Many of his ideas became important references for parenting.

Watson is well known for his experiments with a nine-month-old boy called Albert. Watson would give Albert a furry toy or pet rat to play with, and then he would suddenly make loud banging noises until the baby burst into tears and covered his ears. This was so traumatizing to Albert that Watson later bragged that the boy could be *controlled* by just showing him the furry objects: fear, intimidation, control— now with just the mere sight of a toy.

Finally, in 1946, the tide turned toward more compassionate parenting when pediatrician Benjamin Spock published his influential book, *The Common Sense Guide to Baby and Child Care* (Spock 1946). Reversing the previous centuries of parenting advice, Spock highlighted the importance of emotional closeness between parent and child. "Don't be afraid to kiss your baby when you feel like it," Spock urged mothers and fathers who had been warned for decades to withhold physical affection. Not surprisingly, critics found his work unorthodox and even dangerous, and parents were sincerely confused. Was Spock too liberal? Would such child-centered parenting lead to willful, indulged generations to come? Some were sure his guidance was ill-advised. In Spock's later years, he was accused of creating the "disobedient" generation of baby boomers who refused to go to war in Vietnam and stood up to authority during the Civil Rights Movement.

Thankfully, parenting advice has continued to evolve, but as hopeful as this progress may be, it's slow to reach or influence the typical family. Despite all we know today about raising healthy and confident children, the modeling by parents, grandparents, and generations remains stubbornly powerful and often unconscious. As a result, practices of using threats and physical punishment to correct children are still common.

A lack of information about the fragile nature of a child's sense of well-being, the parenting our parents experienced, the modeling our parents saw, and the stresses of a modern life—all these factors contribute to emphasizing obedience and control.

The American practice of hitting children

Were you ever told, "Stop crying, or I'll give you something to cry about"? According to two researchers, Cuddy and Reeves, writing for the Brookings Institute, "Hitting children is more culturally acceptable in America than in many other nations—not only by parents but teachers too." (Cuddy and Reeves 2014)

Did you know that in sixty-six countries worldwide, the physical punishment of children is outlawed, but not in the United States? Ironically, corporal punishment in all states is not considered assault (as long as it doesn't leave a mark or break the skin), but an adult hitting another adult is assault.

Research clearly shows that any corporal discipline brings on a vicious cycle of escalating poor behavior and then more severe punishment. A large study conducted in twenty of the largest U.S. cities showed that "children who were spanked more than twice a month were more aggressive at subsequent surveys." (Cuddy and Reeves 2014) Even in cases where caring parenting practices occurred in families that also used corporal punishment, the link between harsh discipline and adolescent conduct disorder and depression remained. Physical punishment leaves emotional scars that *aren't erased* by subsequent kind words or caring gestures. In other words, children who were physically punished but are later hugged still suffer. Research also shows that children who are physically punished have slower cognitive development than children whose parents use other methods.

We come from generations of parents who used physical punishment, emotional threats, and verbal abuse to raise their children. This is the context in which our parents learned parenting and where we, if we have children, learned ours. It's unhealthy and damaging, and because we were shamed as children, we talk to ourselves in shaming ways. What else could we say to ourselves when we screw up? Here is where the use of guilt comes in.

Shame versus guilt

Guilt has an abysmal reputation. We have maligned guilt because we haven't understood that shame is our real enemy. Part of the confusion is that guilt and shame have been identified as the same emotion, which they are not.

Shame is one of the survival responses to threat or harm. Shame is a feeling or an assessment of *oneself*. It's an identity: "I feel badly because I *am* bad." With shame, one part of the mind steps aside and judges the other part: stupid, bad, and defective. It's a doubly painful emotion because not only do we label ourselves, but we also believe others perceive us to be how we feel—inferior or unworthy.

Guilt is a feeling of regret about our *behavior*, especially when it violates cultural or religious norms: "I feel bad because I *did* a bad thing." Guilt focuses on how our behavior has affected the other person and leads us to consider what we can do about it.

Shame versus guilt disciplinary practices

Let's identify specific parental behaviors thought to be sources of shame. A group of researchers, including Tangney, identified the following. See if these practices were part of your experience as a child.

Here are examples of shame parenting:

- **Love withdrawal:** "How can I love you when you act like that."
- **Power assertion:** Corporal punishment and dominating behavior such as "do it because I said so." "Go eat on the floor like the pig you are."
- **Parent-focused discipline:** The focus is on the feelings and the consequences for the parent. "Do you understand how much you embarrassed me? What will people think of me now?" "I am so hurt by how you acted. You're so ungrateful for all I do for you."
- **Neglect and ignoring:** "Get away from me." "Don't touch me." "You don't exist to me."
- **Public humiliation in front of peers, family, or strangers:** "Cry baby, Suzie. Look at you. I hope your face doesn't freeze with that look on it."
- **Conditional approval:** "Why should I love a brat that behaves like you do?"
- **Person-focused responses:** "I'm so ashamed of you. What the hell were you thinking."
- **Disgust, teasing, contempt:** "You disgust me. You're just a baby. Big baby."

In contrast, here are examples of guilt-inducing parenting:

- **Victim-focused:** The attention is on the feelings and consequences of the victim. "Look how scared you made Jenny feel."
- **Teaching reparation:** "What can you do to help Jenny feel better?"
- **Behavior-focused responses:** "You need to stop grabbing Bobby's toys. It upsets him and it isn't nice."
- **Other-person-focused responses:** "I want you to think of other people's feelings more."

With guilt, we can focus on correcting behavior, apologizing, and learning how to make reparations. In contrast, shame makes us feel terrible about ourselves and fosters defensiveness, anger, retaliation, and blaming—quite a difference.

Guilt and empathy

Earlier, we discussed the importance of empathy and how shame-prone people are low on empathy. Because guilt focuses on how our behavior has hurt the other person, it encourages empathy. A mother can tell her young daughter, "Jenny doesn't like it when you grab her doll from her. Look at how upset she is. Is there anything you can do to help Jenny feel better?" Research shows that a child will have developed enough empathy by age four to know how Jenny feels. The child is aware when her behavior isn't kind. Therefore, a child's natural empathy can be encouraged by asking them to imagine how another is feeling. With this type of guidance, children increase their awareness of their innate empathic feelings toward others, and this empathy grows.

By talking with the child about what harm was done and assisting them to devise appropriate strategies to take reparative action, children learn to problem-solve and develop their capacity to think through the process of making amends. This is far more helpful than saying, "Give your sister a hug, and tell her you love her." When parents help children build a repertoire of possible actions, kids gradually become better at thinking up their own amends.

Below is a chart comparing shame and guilt as it relates to empathy.

Situation	Shame	Guilt
Has empathy for another	Interferes or blocks	Yes
Thinks of others before acting	No	Yes
Imagines how others see him and sees himself that way	Yes	No
Curbs socially inappropriate behavior	No	Yes
Is inclined to blame others	Yes	No
Knows ways to make amends	No	Yes
Focuses on their own distress rather than another's distress	Yes	No

Adapted from Tangney and Dearing (2002)

Linking our behavior to our self-worth—that is, "what's wrong with me?"—suggests that we're the sum total of our behaviors. But as we know, we're all a mixture of good and bad behaviors, and our worth is established not by our actions but by our very existence. Nothing comes broken from heaven. Everyone comes into life loving and lovable.

Our culture has historically linked bad behavior with being a bad person. Many think that when someone makes a number of bad choices, they morph into a bad person. Think of your judgments about people on the evening news who have committed some terrible crime. Do you think they're bad people, or do you think they did some horrible acts? If you're like the majority, you tend to equate bad mistakes with being a bad person.

We have also falsely believed that children and adults will stop making further bad choices if they're adequately shamed. But the research of Tangney and Dearing tells a different story. *Shame doesn't deter wrongdoing.* Shamed individuals are more likely to become angry and defensive, and to act out aggressively—either passive-aggressively, like stealing or using drugs, or with direct aggression, like committing domestic violence, fighting, and murder. (Tangney and Dearing 2002).

Are shame-prone kids destined to make poor choices? Research demonstrates a direct link between a child's upbringing with shame versus guilt and the choices they make growing up. One study followed 380 children from racially diverse, high school-educated parents in the Washington, D.C., area. They were first given a battery of psychological tests when they were in the fifth grade. The findings showed that children's propensity to behave in ways consistent with being guilt-prone or shame-prone was well-established by the fifth grade. Eight years later, these same children were interviewed again, and their behaviors corresponded to whether they were guilt-prone or shame-prone. "The pattern is pretty clear cut," write Tangney and Dearing. "Guilt is good. Shame is bad."

A summary of their findings is in the chart below. Children who were corrected using guilt were significantly better adjusted. Those of us who are shame-prone have a significant disadvantage. We could say we didn't have a chance.

Shame-prone	Guilt-prone
High incidents of hard drug use	Not likely to use hard drugs
Likely criminal behavior	Criminal behavior unlikely
Risky sexual behavior	Fewer sexual partners; more safe sex
Less likely to engage in community service	Likely to engage in community service
More high school suspensions	Apply to college
Begin drinking at an early age	If used, alcohol use began in late teens or early adulthood
Less able to empathize with others	Able to empathize with others
Prone to blame others	Accepts responsibility

Higher incidence of domestic violence	Higher levels of psychological well-being
More inclined to suicide	Suicide and suicidal ideation rare
It affects more women than men	Men predisposed to guilt
More dysfunction in the family	Better communication, conflict resolution
Vulnerable to depression	No increased vulnerability to depression
Does not inhibit problematic behavior	Inhibits problematic behavior

Guilt-tripping ourselves

When we make a mistake, such as doing something foolish, hurting someone's feelings, or yelling too much at our children, we have a choice about how we think and feel about ourselves. Even though shame-prone people will habitually go into a shame reaction and see themselves as bad people (bad mother, bad friend, etc.), we can also pause and go down a different path. Making a conscious shift to focus on your *behavior* as the problem puts you squarely in guilt territory. Making this shift takes practice and patience.

We don't want to hurt or offend other people, but occasionally we will. Now, we have some choices. Instead of slumping into a shame spiral, justifying our behavior, blaming the other person for being too sensitive, or walking away in a huff, we can remember that *we made a mistake*. You are not a bad person, but you owe the other person an apology. This is hard for many shame-prone people, but generally, you can sincerely feel, "I'm sorry. I didn't mean to hurt your feelings" (or upset you, disappoint you, let you down, or betray you).

Avoid the habit of making excuses or explanations. Instead, make a clean, sincere apology, and then pause. If they start to tell you what a thoughtless person you are or any other accusing label, hear them out. When you are making an apology, it isn't the time to defend or argue your case. That may come much later.

Finally, what can you do to make amends? As an adult, this isn't as simple as buying someone a new toy truck because we broke theirs. Instead, you may need to make many amends, or you may be unsure of what you can do. You can ask, "What can I do, if anything, to make this better?" Making amends or reparations is an apology in action. And, though words can be cheap, they're also essential. Those we have hurt need our words of apology and our efforts.

Should we apologize to our children if we have mistreated them? Yes. My nephew, who is the father of a ten-year-old, shared an incident in which his son cursed him during an argument. Incensed, the father grabbed the son, put soap in his mouth, and shoved him into a cold shower. The father did not feel good about how he had disciplined his son. He knew he had punished out of anger, but he also confided that he didn't know what else to do. I suggested he tell his son he felt terrible about how he handled the situation and apologize. By doing this, the father shows his child that parents are humans who make mistakes, and apologizing is what one does when that happens. Maybe the son will also apologize at some later date. Who knows? But the modeling he has seen is that everyone deserves an apology when we mistreat them.

We need to befriend guilt. We have a choice. We can stop shaming our kids *and ourselves* and instead focus on repairing our hurtful behaviors and making amends. Be the one who stops the generational practice of shaming. Let it end with you.

Next, we will explore one of the ways the mind deals with overwhelming stress. Since this level of stress or, in some incidents, terror often starts with how we were parented, it is an appropriate next chapter.

Chapter Takeaways

1. Parenting practices involving shame have been passed down through generations to socialize and teach obedience. Historically, a child's emotional well-being has not been appreciated as significantly as we know it is today.

2. Parents learn how to parent by modeling how they were parented.

3. In the United States, hitting children is more culturally acceptable than in many other nations, even though we have research that shows that the consequences of corporal punishment are devastating to children's well-being.

4. For many, not using shaming to correct oneself or others requires learning other alternatives.

5. Shame focuses on one's identity, making a person feel bad about who they are. Guilt focuses on behavior and its consequences.

6. Research shows that guilt-prone (versus shame-prone) individuals are more likely to make positive changes in their behavior, demonstrate empathy, and develop greater self-acceptance.

7. Shame-prone individuals are more inclined toward anger, defensiveness, and problematic behavior.

8. By choosing guilt over shame and teaching children how to make amends for their actions, parents, teachers, coaches, and church leaders can break the cycle of generations of shaming and promote healthier emotional growth in their children.

9. Guilt allows one to see themself as a human being who makes mistakes, not as a bad person.

Reflection Question

When you watch the news and hear about someone who has committed repeated crimes, does the distinction between bad behavior and a bad person challenge how you have typically thought of these offenders?

Practice

Notebook in hand:

1. Write a brief summary of a situation where you did something wrong—thoughtless or even cruel—and thought a shame-based judgment of yourself, such as "you are such a scum bag."

2. Now think of the same situation and say, "That was a really poorly thought-out choice you made."

3. How does that feel?

4. Next time you make a mistake or regret some choice you make, use some guilt on yourself (by commenting on your behavior not your whole self) and see if it makes a difference. Using guilt-type phrases takes practice, but once you stop shaming yourself, you won't feel good going back to doing so.

8

A Mind Fragmented by Trauma

There are things in the psyche which I do not produce but which produce themselves and have their own lives.

—Carl Jung

Have you ever experienced being "taken over" by a part of yourself that you didn't know was there? "I don't know what got into me," you might say, reflecting on your behavior. Or you've been aware of a disagreement between two parts of you: "One part of me thinks I should just tell that SOB boss to shove it, but another part of me thinks that would be stupid because I need a job and maybe he had a point."

How do we explain these incidents of "two minds"? Remember the metaphor of an angel on one shoulder and the devil on the other? As psychologists explored the origins and causes of these "many minds," researchers and therapists observed that the mind naturally has subpersonalities, parts, or ego states.

The "many selves" phenomenon, we now know, is universal and normal, and it occurs in everyone. Although many theories exist, we don't understand how the mind creates the parts. But one thing most researchers agree on is that we aren't one mind; instead, we're a collection of "parts" that have specific functions, feelings, and thoughts. Even everyday life, with all its challenges, creates parts. The difference is that these parts are not disowned or exiled. For example, you may have parent parts, career parts, or dancer parts. These parts are like specialists that contribute to a functioning human being. In contrast, the parts of us created by trauma are aspects of our mind that are still lost in the trauma and continue to suffer. These parts created by trauma are the most challenging and the most in need of healing.

While the creation of subpersonalities or parts does not require trauma, this "ability" is particularly critical in situations of trauma—especially childhood abuse and neglect. What constitutes trauma? "Trauma isn't simply what happens to us. It's what goes on inside us. Trauma is a wound that happens inside us, leading to a belief that I'm not worthy because if I were worthy, this bad thing wouldn't be happening to me." (Mate 2023) Trauma is any situation or experience that is beyond the child's (or adult's) ability to process emotionally and to recover. Situations like these leave the child emotionally overwhelmed and terrified. It can be an ongoing situation, such as living with a primary parent who is emotionally and physically abusive or neglectful; or an event such as the premature death of a parent or being physically attacked.

Many psychologists now believe that in traumatic situations, the mind splits off into parts and keeps these parts out of conscious awareness, allowing the traumatized child to continue functioning. All parts that are split off because of trauma are stuck in a time warp, unaware that life has moved on. They do not know that they may no longer be in danger. For them, life is as it was when they lived in trauma.

More about "parts"

A "part" carries the trauma's memory, affect, and beliefs, thereby protecting the mind from being totally fractured and overwhelmed. If some part of the trauma does break through into awareness, the part is disowned: "It's not me." That is, the terror of what happened is explained by "it didn't happen to me." This allows the non-traumatized self-parts to distance themselves from the feelings and knowledge of the abuse—and to keep on going. This adaptive genius allows the traumatized child to carry on as though no trauma has occurred. For example, the child who has been sexually abused the night before can join the family for breakfast while the abusive father sits across the table. The abuse memories and pain are split off from awareness. This allows the child to feel some attachment to their abusive parent and to enjoy every morsel of kindness and acceptance available to her. In this way, children aren't just survivors, but, as Janina Fisher says in her book, *Healing the Fragmented Selves of Trauma Survivors* (Fisher 2017), they are "ingenious survivors." This is nature's way of ensuring survival.

In many cases, the greater the trauma, the more the trauma-filled parts are disowned. They are out of awareness, or any sense of them is vague ("they're not me"). Nowhere is this more important than when early lives are filled with the trauma that causes fear-induced shame that the child could not otherwise endure.

When "parts" break through into awareness

When something happens in the current (adult) life that in some way resonates with the part's experience of their trauma, the part pops into our present-day awareness. For example, many adults who were sexually abused as children have great difficulty when they are sexual. To their dismay, unbidden memories and feelings of child parts break through into the adult's awareness. They may find that they are terrified, repulsed, and angry—these responses to the current situations are the same as when they were children. Their attitudes, behaviors, beliefs, and problem-solving are no different than they were years ago. These parts are stuck in the past and remain at the developmental level where they were when they were created.

I learned about this ingenious survival strategy firsthand when I began working with a client who, unbeknownst to me then, had been severely abused as a child. Her situation is an extreme example of parts, because her abuse was severe, but it's also one that shows how this phenomenon of splitting off parts keeps us safe and functioning.

In the mid-1980s, a decade into my career, I worked with a thirty-five-year-old married woman whom I'll call Dorothy. During the first month that we worked together, our sessions centered on her marriage and work situation. But as we spent more time together, she began to talk about her early life, and as she did, she would suddenly take on the mannerisms of a terrified child. Then, almost like she was in a trance, she would get up from her chair and crouch in the corner of my office, cowering with terror from some unknown source.

I would try to get her to realize the safety of the here and now, but she was too frightened to absorb my efforts to soothe and reassure her. Eventually, Dorothy would emerge from her terrifying world and return to her chair. When I asked her what had just happened, she had no recollection and looked genuinely baffled and afraid.

I was baffled too and consulted several colleagues. As therapists, we had all worked with clients who "regressed" to childlike states, but my colleagues and I didn't understand why Dorothy didn't remember these episodes. Then, one day, as I was wrapping up a session while Dorothy sat slumped in depression in her chair, she suddenly changed posture, sat up straight, and looked me in the eyes. Then she asked in a voice I didn't recognize, "Who are you?"

"Holy cow!" I thought as fear washed over me. Then I introduced myself.

"I know who you are," the voice replied. "I'm Sarah, and I'm here to introduce you to the inside children. We figured I should come and tell you about them because you didn't seem to be figuring it out on your own." She was right. A few days before meeting Sarah, I had been reading through the *Diagnostic and Statistical Manual,* the book of diagnostic criteria that therapists use, trying to find an explanation for Dorothy's behavior. When I came to the chapter on Multiple Personality Disorder, I remember flipping on to the next chapter while saying aloud to myself, "No one believes in that stuff"—which, at that time, was predominately true.

However, as I met and learned about these "inner children," who ranged in age from young toddlers to teenagers and adults, I became convinced of the reality of this adaptive process of splitting off parts. This process saved Dorothy's life, allowing her to get an education, marry, have children, and function in a career.

Tich Nhat Hanh, the late respected Zen Buddhist master, spoke about how we all have inner children. In his book, *Reconciliation: Healing the Inner Child,* he wrote, "we have all had pain in our childhoods, some more than others, and there remain parts of us that are cut off from the love and compassion that such pain deserves and needs." While we're generally unaware of this, "the wounded child is always there trying to get our attention. But because we are afraid of the suffering (we may encounter as we process these feelings), we run away and distract ourselves with 'life.' This child has been severely wounded. She needs us to return." (Hanh 2010)

This unconscious process of sequestering painful sensations, memories, and beliefs into what feels like inner children or subpersonalities is similar to how our body builds barriers around injured or infected tissue. Like our bodies, our minds create semi-permeable amnesiac barriers around emotional trauma, so the conscious mind isn't directly aware of the parts that hold the pain of abandonment or abuse. While the splitting off of parts that hold the trauma is an important safety mechanism to shield the child from the effects of the trauma, as adults our goal is to befriend those suffering young parts and help them process what happened so they can heal. We will explore the details of a process for healing in the next chapter.

Parts don't just go away

When the unhealed younger parts of our minds take over and attempt to use their own survival strategies and childlike methods to handle adult situations, these younger aspects of ourselves can't help but act as we did as children. For example, when your boss is sexually inappropriate and "pats" you on the bottom, your younger parts may be triggered, but they can't respond as an adult would. Instead, you may find yourself laughing, giggling, speechless, frozen, or just ignoring the situation. Likewise, when we encounter upsetting everyday challenges, instead of bringing an adult self to the task, we may be flooded with inept childlike coping strategies. We might rage, cry, beg, or become mute. This unbidden takeover by a part of us can be humiliating, causing us to feel crazy and weird. But we are not crazy—we are under the influence of a traumatized part that needs our adult self's help.

Considering that it's challenging to make good adult decisions even under the best circumstances, when parts of our personality system are immature, traumatized, and emotionally unmoored, our choices and behaviors can be particularly regrettable. It's important to remember that we didn't choose to act in these ways. It's the price we pay for unhealed, traumatized parts within us that may have saved us in the past but need our healing focus now.

Understandably, we want to eliminate this onslaught of impulses, moods, beliefs, and attitudes that affect our lives now. But we must be careful. If we turn against our parts and become angry with them, we also turn against ourselves, because they were—and are—us. We may not realize that by hating our parts, we re-traumatize and abandon the parts of ourselves that helped us survive and now need our understanding and compassion.

As challenging as this may seem, we also have a unique strength. As a number of therapists working with trauma-filled parts have discovered, we all have a part that's unaffected by trauma. I knew this part for Dorothy as Jacqueline, and I thought of her as a guardian angel. Others refer to this as the Wise Mind, the Higher Self, or the Self part. This aspect is available to all of us. We recognize this aspect because it is always caring and nonjudgmental. We may not have much access to that essence now, but as we heal the childlike parts that carry the trauma, they become less emotionally distraught and intrusive, and, as a result, we begin to experience a quieter emotional inner world. This allows us greater access to this unseen guidance and source of self-accepting love.

We are *all inherently multiple,* which helps explain the paradoxical feelings, impulses, and points of view we all experience. In the healing section of this book, I describe a process that I learned to use with Dorothy and have used many times with myself and other clients. I also learned from Richard Schwartz, founder of Internal Family System, processes for healing parts, and I incorporate his extraordinarily helpful insights and strategies into my processes. As we heal our parts, we will see that they are our courageous and suffering little superheroes.

Chapter Takeaways

1. Our minds are not singular entities; rather, they are naturally composed of various subpersonalities, or parts with distinct functions, feelings, and thoughts.
2. Traumatic experiences, especially in childhood, can lead to the creation of many parts within the mind. These parts hold the memories, emotions, and beliefs associated with the trauma. They served to protect us by keeping these painful aspects out of our conscious awareness.
3. When these traumatized parts resurface in adulthood due to triggers or similar situations, they may cause us to react as we did during the traumatic experience. Understanding and healing these parts is crucial to resolving these reactions and allowing us to respond from an adult perspective.
4. Despite the presence of traumatized parts, there is also an unaffected, compassionate Self, or inner being, within everyone. This Self remains nonjudgmental and serves as a source of wisdom and love. Healing the traumatized parts can lead to greater access to this essential aspect of ourselves.

Reflection Question

Reflect on the statement, "we are all multiple." Does it help you understand your seemingly opposite or contradictory feelings, thoughts, and even behavior?

Practice

Notebook in hand:

1. Have you ever experienced a situation in which an inner self from your past took over inappropriately in your current adult life?
2. How did you feel toward this part at the time?
3. How has the information in this chapter helped you understand what that situation may have been?
4. Might you feel differently toward that part in the future?

PART 2

HEALING OUR WOUNDS

Introduction

The wound is the place where the Light enters you.

—Rumi

We are the wounded survivors of a heartbroken past. Many times, it may appear that shame had the upper hand and our wounds would never heal. But while shame is a formidable force, we are all born with the resources needed for our healing. There is a well-trodden path for us to follow on our healing journey. *We're never too old or too broken.*

We will begin by learning a process for healing our wounded inner parts. Because of the scorching pain of shame's labels—unlovable, unworthy, and not good enough—we have hated ourselves, harmed ourselves, and sometimes tried to destroy ourselves. We have exiled and turned against parts of ourselves because we didn't know what else to do. But these traumatized parts need us to befriend them and offer them the healing they deserve. After all, they are the brave children of our past who did one hell of a job getting us where we are today. We can learn how to lead them out of the time warp they are in and bring them home, into our hearts.

Shame has also interfered with our relationships with other people. And it's no wonder! We've been betrayed, abused, ignored, and humiliated by those we needed and trusted to love us. How can we ever trust again? We fear getting too close. We can't take any more disappointment or betrayal, yet we feel lonely and unseen.

We can learn how to identify and choose trustworthy people in our lives, and when we do so, we can encourage ourselves to gradually let our vulnerable selves be touched by the caring of the safe people around us—even just one or two. We can teach ourselves the life skills of self-compassion, self-soothing, and self-forgiveness, skills we need to survive the roller coaster of life.

We're all born with an innate drive for growth and wholeness—to become who we are. An acorn will always become an oak. This inner push often feels like discontent. But this discontent is a life force that pushes us, while the inspiration of hope simultaneously beckons us to pick ourselves up, survey our injuries, and begin the journey to healing. We can confidently believe in these natural forces because they are a law of nature.

Nothing comes broken from heaven. Everyone comes into life loving and lovable. You may not feel that way, but you were born worthy of love and acceptance. Nothing has changed that. Nothing your parents, caretakers, or abusers have said or done could change who you really are. Nothing you have done or said has changed who you are, either. You were injured, not damaged. You were hurt, not bad. You were *Bruised Not Broken*. And your hurts and injuries can heal.

Along the way, you'll find fellow travelers who will teach, inspire, encourage, and rest with you when you're weary. I'm one of those. There are thousands more. So, let's begin our first steps on the path to healing. I will lead the way.

9

Befriending the Parts of Our Selves That Are Stuck in the Past

To learn how to listen to our parts entails a radical leap of faith and a willingness to believe that our distressing feelings, thoughts, behaviors, impulses, images, and dreams represent communications from parts.

—Janina Fisher

Earlier we learned that we are not of one mind, but rather, little discreet parts or sub-personalities. (These terms are used interchangeably.) These parts communicate and influence us in ways that we may not recognize. Abuse, rejection, and neglect are such excruciating experiences to our young selves that these traumas cannot be metabolized and are instead split off to save the larger mind. These split-off aspects become our parts. The feelings of shame and the beliefs that originated during those painful experiences remain unchanged in our parts' psychology. Eventually, these aspects are triggered by current experiences, and their content and emotions spill into our awareness. When we don't realize they are communications from parts, we are baffled and often distressed.

"We have ongoing, complex relationships with the many different inner voices, thought patterns, and emotions. What we call thinking is often our inner dialogues with different parts of us." (Schwartz 2001) Here's an example.

My close friend, Ann, had been unable to shake a chronic sinus inflammation despite months of antibiotics and other interventions. As a result, she was discouraged and depressed. Her acupuncturist, whom she liked and trusted, suggested her ailments may have an emotional component and recommended she do some "inner child" work. But Ann was reluctant and said she didn't know how.

Ann knew I had done personal and professional work with this mysterious "inner child" phenomenon, but she declined when I offered to help her with the process. I persisted and told her how significant it had been in my healing process. Finally, she agreed.

I asked her to sit quietly for a few minutes, focus on her body, and see if she was aware of any particular feelings. After a few minutes in which we were both silent, she said she felt sadness in her chest.

"Where is the sadness coming from?" I asked.

Slowly, she replied, "A little me."

"Good. Can you see her?"

"Yes, she has on a pretty, blue coat, and I think she's waiting to go somewhere. She's twirling now, so I can see her coat. It's lovely."

"Why don't you say hello and ask her how she's feeling."

"She's telling me she's sad because no one loves her."

Then I heard Ann say, "Of course, someone loves you. Look at the beautiful coat you have. Someone loved you enough to buy that for you."

"Whoa!" I thought. Over the years, I had often heard Ann say she grew up getting things when she really wanted time and attention from her parents.

I suggested Ann put her hand on her heart and breathe through her hand, taking in a few slow breaths. Then, I suggested she ask the little girl about not feeling loved. "She's telling me that she likes her coat, but she feels lonely and sad," Ann told me. "Now, she's asking me if she can touch my hair." Ann's hair had always been an issue because her mother didn't know what to do with her very curly blond locks. There were many trips to salons to get it straightened. Now, as an adult, Ann had let it go naturally curly.

She continued to talk with her young self, and she described their conversation. Young Ann told Adult Ann that she often felt lonely and that no one cared about her.

After a few more minutes sitting together silently, Ann said she had nothing more to say and wanted to end the encounter. Before she did, however, I heard her spontaneously say, "I'll come back, and we can talk some more. I want you to know that I love you."

Ann told me she had returned to visit her inner little girl several more times over the next few weeks: "I listened to her tell me how she tried to hide her sad feelings because her parents didn't like a sad girl. But it didn't seem to matter." The little girl told Ann that she didn't know why her parents didn't like her. "She asked me if I would spend time with her," Ann reported. "I couldn't believe how candid she was—open and delightful. As she talked, we often cried together. So now, I just carry her around with me and talk to her. I know that sounds silly, but that's what I do. She loves it, and so do I."

"When I'm aware that I'm feeling sad and unloved, I know that my little self needs more attention from me," Ann told me. "I used to think I needed someone else to show me more love or attention. And while this may be true also, it's clear to me that deep healing needs to come from me."

Ann's sinus issues gradually cleared up, and soon she was symptom-free. Was it because she had befriended and showed compassion for the little Ann she encountered? We don't know, but something shifted. And because the mind and body are connected, the act of compassion toward ourselves is healing for the body.

Ann hadn't deliberately looked for her inner child; instead, she was distressed by sinus issues. Sometimes we become aware of unhealed aspects of our younger selves through body sensations and illnesses. Other times, we're overtaken by childish impulses, scenes, or snippets from our past that push into our awareness when we are tired, stressed, or emotionally untethered. Whatever the source, becoming aware that we have childlike parts that carry pain or worry is an opportunity to heal our past selves.

Hijacked

We never know what will activate our inner parts, but relationships with those we care about, such as a sweetheart, often touch issues and wounds that bring our parts into our awareness. These are the parts that absorbed the wounding of our early lives, when our primary caretakers failed us in ways that were too painful for us to tolerate. When these parts break through, it can be very distressing—but if we understand what is happening, it becomes an opportunity to heal those same parts, which need our healing attention.

When my friend, Marilyn, called me one afternoon. I could hear the distress in her voice. "I know you've done a lot of work on yourself," she said, "and I need some help." Through her tears, she explained that she was scared she was blowing up a relationship that meant a lot to her. "I'm so clingy and jealous, and that just isn't me. I can't control it. I'm scared." I knew how much her new relationship meant to her. She had been divorced for twenty years after two unhappy marriages, and even venturing into dating had been a brave, monumental step. After months of unsuccessful dating, she finally met Chris and called to tell me how smitten she was. But as any meaningful relationship entails emotional vulnerability, it often brings up emotional wounds from our first relationship—the one with our parents.

Marilyn told me that after six happy months of dating, Chris's mother had fallen and broken her hip. Since he was the only local family member, he suddenly needed to spend a lot of time with his elderly mother. Marilyn completely understood and respected his kind thoughtfulness, but it also meant less time for them together. To her surprise, she began to feel desperation and anxiety that she didn't understand. "I wait for him to call me and worry if he doesn't, even though he just called me the night before. I feel anxious so much of the time. Sometimes I'm cold when he does call and I'm sullen and don't want to talk. And when he comes to see me, I feel distant and don't want to be physically close to him. Poor guy! I'm driving him nuts, and I'm scared I'll lose this relationship. Kristine, this just isn't me—except it is. I've done a lot of inner work too, but I just can't shake this pattern."

Knowing that Marilyn was familiar with inner child work, I said, "Marilyn, let's talk to this part of you that feels so desperate. Can you see her?"

Marilyn began to sob. "Yes, she's so little, and she's trying to wake up her daddy." Her voice now sounded young and scared. "Daddy, I'm hungry. Please wake up and feed me. I'm hungry, Daddy." Finally, Marilyn's voice became adult. "Oh my god! It's that little part of me that stayed with my alcoholic father while my mother went to work. I had no idea what that was like. She's so hungry and scared. No one is taking care of her. Now she's going to the kitchen, but she can't find any food to eat." Then Marilyn explained that when her mother finally did come home, she'd be so mad at her husband for drinking all day that they would argue and fight. "My mother wasn't available either. She was always mad. I found my father dead when I was five, you know."

I remembered that Marilyn had lost her father at age five, but at that moment, I was concerned that she had disconnected emotionally from her child part. "Marilyn," I said, "let's return to your young self. Can you still see her?"

"Yes, she's standing alone in the living room. She seems upset with me."

"Would you like to invite her to come and sit with you?"

Marilyn did, but the younger part of her said, "No." I suggested that Marilyn tell her it was okay.

"Now, she's moving toward me," Marilyn said, "but she's sitting away from me with her back toward me. Wow! That's just how I am with Chris. I want to be close, but I'm mad too. I think I hurt her feelings when I started talking to you instead of paying attention to her. 'I'm sorry. I think I hurt your feelings.' She nodded."

I suggested that Marilyn ask the little girl to show her what her young life is like. "Tell her you can see the pictures in her mind, and you want to know about her life." Marilyn described how her young self showed her a place where her daddy would take her when he saw his friends. She got to sit on a big stool and have a special drink. She liked that, but her daddy didn't talk to her, and she felt very lonely and a little scared.

Marilyn fell silent and then told me that her little self appeared calmer and just faded away. "Wow, that was potent," she told me. "I learned to do something like that when I was in therapy, but mostly, I did all the talking, reassuring that little girl and telling her she was safe. I guess I never really asked her questions or invited her to talk about her life or worries. And I never felt her viscerally. This time, I could feel I was her. You helped me listen to her, and she needed a voice."

A week later, I talked to Marilyn again. "I've talked with my little girl several times," she said. "I made time, as you suggested, and spent as much time with her as she wanted. I mostly listened and watched little Marilyn show me what her day-to-day life was like. There were many times when I cried, and she seemed surprised. I think she wasn't used to someone caring about her feelings."

"Many more memories have opened up," Marilyn continued. "I can see that the behaviors and feelings I've had with Chris are coming from her. But I just listen to her, and sometimes we just sit together. You know, eventually, she sat right next to me, and I could feel her with me. I told her she can talk to me and show me things anytime she wants. And, get this—I don't feel as desperate and anxious with Chris as I did! Of course, I would like to see him more, but I'm mostly in my adult self with him. I understand that his mother needs him and he isn't choosing his mother over me. He's just taking care of her like a good son."

Marilyn and Ann had begun the process of bringing their young parts out of isolation and into their conscious awareness by befriending them. As Janina Fisher (the respected pioneer in trauma treatment that I mentioned previously) said, "we befriend them the same way we would befriend anyone. We show interest and curiosity—we want to know what makes the other person tick—their likes, dislikes, fears, fantasies, habits, and growing edges. This means listening, really hearing them." (Fisher 2017)

Sometimes, however, that isn't so easy to do. For example, my client, Robin, was a successful professional, respected and sought out by colleagues who trusted her advice and help. This success didn't ease the haunting self-doubt she felt in her personal life. She had told me many times about how invisible she felt—like she didn't matter. Despite her successful career, her enduring friendships, and the love of her children, feelings of emptiness occupied her. "What's wrong with me?" she would exclaim out of frustration.

One day, as Robin talked about a painful incident in which she felt ignored by her sisters, I asked her to focus on the "I don't matter" feeling to see if she could find where it came from. She sat quietly for a few minutes and said, "I see a younger version of myself hiding behind the corner of a building. I think she's waiting for her mother." Robin had many memories of being left at school into the evening before her mother or father picked her up. She felt so humiliated waiting at the curb that she hid behind a building to prevent teachers and kids from seeing her. Even though one of her parents eventually picked her up, what was she to think? Did she matter? Had they forgotten about her? Maybe they couldn't be bothered. She felt like she wasn't important to them.

When I asked Robin to look more closely at her young self, a critical part was triggered. She said, "Look at her. She looks so pathetic. She should be used to it. Besides, they always eventually come for her." Then, Robin told her younger part, "Buck up, girl. Get over it!"

Approaching our parts as we would a stranger

Robin needed some help to bypass her critical part. Taking a less direct approach, I suggested to Robin that she imagine the little girl as a stranger—someone she saw when she picked up her own children from school. I asked her what she'd feel if it was late in the afternoon and she saw a little girl waiting alone and worried. Might she say something to her? What would it be? I hoped Robin's compassion as a mother raising her children would kick in.

Robin said she would offer to call the girl's parents and to wait with her until they arrived. Then, to my surprise, she began to talk directly to her own little girl part. The inner girl told her how scared and embarrassed she was. "No one cares about me," she said to Robin. "But I don't want anyone to know. It's a secret."

"How do you feel towards her?" I asked Robin.

"She reminds me of myself when I was younger. Maybe she is me. I feel sad for her."

Sometimes, we're simply not ready to directly contact a younger self. Our critical, fearful adult self is in the way. I was frankly surprised that Robin was able to interact with her younger self so compassionately after such a critical first encounter.

Some of my colleagues and friends are skeptical when I tell them about helping clients meet younger parts of themselves. Some don't believe there's any reality to the inner parts healing process, and others can't imagine that anyone could so easily and readily make contact. Let me assure you that I am convinced of the validity of this healing process because of my professional and personal experiences, some of which I have shared. And as to the ease of making these contacts, it varies for everyone. Some may find that this is not a process that works for them. Other processes such as EMDR or art therapy may be more helpful. But if you find yourself drawn to inner child work, as it is called, be patient, sit quietly, ask to meet who is behind the feelings, sensations, or fears you are experiencing, and just wait. Your meeting may seem like only your imagination, or you may have only a vague sense of a younger aspect that you can't see as much as sense. But if you suspend your desire for a concrete encounter and talk with this aspect as you would a shy and retiring child, you may find that you have actually made contact with an inner aspect of yourself who is eager to share with you.

It isn't difficult to understand why we might resent our inner parts. We often first encounter them when they inconveniently intrude in our lives. We can experience their feelings and behaviors as confusing, foreign, weird, or even embarrassing. For example, we may be in an intimate moment with someone we like and suddenly become very frightened and panicked. We may feel humiliated if we are too afraid to stand up for ourselves when we are mistreated. We might say, "Buck up!" as Robin said, or "Stop being so pathetic." But we know those attitudes aren't healing and are likely even damaging. Remember that these internal parts are innocent aspects of us who took direct hits from our caretakers or others and still did their job of holding our pain so that we could go on with our sanity intact. They are heroes.

Chapter Takeaways

1. We all have inner parts, or subpersonalities, that are a normal phenomenon shaped by our experiences. Acknowledging and understanding these parts is one way to understand ourselves and to heal.
2. Our distressing feelings, thoughts, behaviors, impulses, images, and dreams often represent communications from parts.
3. Traumatic experiences, whether physical or emotional, create deep emotional wounds and beliefs that remain unchanged in our inner parts' psychology. When these unhealed parts resurface in response to current experiences, their behavior and beliefs can be distressing and childlike.
4. Relationships, especially ones in which we feel emotionally vulnerable, can trigger unhealed inner parts. Being hijacked by our inner parts is uncomfortable and sometimes embarrassing.

5. Developing compassion and empathy for our inner parts, even when their feelings and behaviors seem challenging, is a crucial step toward healing and wholeness.

Reflection Question

How does the concept of "parts" and how they influence our thoughts and behaviors help you understand yourself better?

Practice

Look through some photos of yourself as a child. They may be photos of inner parts that are still "alive" in your psyche. Write your thoughts in your notebook:

1. Are you with other family members? Look at each one and ask yourself how you feel about them.
2. Who are you standing next to? Does anyone have their arm around you? Do you feel emotionally close to anyone?
3. What facial expressions do you have? Is there sadness beneath your smile? Frowning?
4. What is your posture?
5. What would you like to tell the little person in those photos?

10

Healing Your Inner Parts

When the client "adopted" or came to love their hurt, lost, and lonely parts, something remarkable happened. Their self-disparagement, self-hatred, and disconnection began spontaneously to yield to self-compassion. And as they developed internal attachment relationships to these young selves, I could see them healing.

—Janina Fisher

In this chapter, we will detail a process for contacting and engaging in healing dialogues with our distressed inner child parts. This is the same process I used with Ann and Marilyn; it is basic, uncomplicated and something you can do on your own.

But a word of caution. If you have ever had suicidal, or homicidal ideation or behaviors, I recommend that you consult a professional and do not try this process on your own. Likewise, self-harming, addictive, or eating-disordered behaviors indicate that you need to work with a therapist specifically trained in trauma therapy. These behaviors are from extremely distressed parts and knowing how to safely and effectively work with them is critical to your healing. They are not bad parts, but they can have dangerous behaviors. Another caution: if at any time you find that you "come to" and don't know what happened or you "lose time" and don't have a continuous timeline of what's been happening, consult a professional. These are all indications that your parts carry highly distressing experiences, and working with the support of someone who knows how to guide and pace this work is important for the healing you deserve.

What is the purpose of your encounters with your wounded inner child parts? To unburden the young part who carries pain, feelings, and beliefs from their past. How do children unburden? By telling an adult what happened while having the adult listen, accept what they are telling them without question, and show genuine compassion for the child's feelings. This is key.

As you are talking to your inner child part, be sure to acknowledge their feelings and experiences. "This must have been a terrible experience." "No wonder you felt so hurt." "No one should be treated like that." "How terrible that you couldn't tell anyone and had to carry these painful feelings all by yourself." To a child who may feel responsible for their mistreatment, you might say, "It sounds like you may feel responsible for what happened to you. Is that correct? Well, I don't think you were. No child is ever responsible for being mistreated." You might also ask them, "How has this been for you to share this with me?" "Do you feel like I understood?" Your intention in asking these questions is to extend compassion and to demonstrate to the child that they have an ally—you—and are no longer alone. Your perspective as a caring adult is essential and can be healing, but your inner child part, like that of any child who has been betrayed and lied to, may not believe you. That's okay. Even as adults, friends may tell us we are not to blame, and it may take us time to accept their perspective.

If you are trying to engage an inner child part and instead you encounter an angry part or a part that is rude and demeaning, you have likely encountered a part of your defense system that is best worked with in the company of someone who is experienced with these parts. The Internal Family Systems (IFS) therapy model provides valuable insight into the purpose of these parts and how they are trying to protect the wounded inner children, but this can be complicated. Working with these challenging parts can be unsettling and even dangerous. I strongly recommend that you consult a professional.

Bringing our parts home

Another step in healing your wounded inner child parts is uniting them with your current life. A big part of their pain is the isolation they have felt. Remember that they are unaware that life has moved on. Stuck in their traumatic past, they do not know there is an adult who can give them the safety and protection they didn't have. Learning that you live in an untroubled home and that they can join you there is like a dream they never expected.

When you're ready, invite them to join you in your life. Some parts will readily accept, while others remain cautious or even refuse. "What do you need to feel safe coming with me into my safe life?" you can ask. At every turn, you will need to be respectful and understand that your inner parts, who have been deeply betrayed, need certain things in order to trust again. We ask what that is, and then we offer it if we can provide it.

With Ann and Marilyn, the trauma was the shame of what was missing. However, if your trauma was abusive or ongoing, you may find the emotions and wounding of your inner parts overwhelming. If you encounter a part or a scene from your past that overwhelms you or makes you feel lost in the memory, STOP. Bring yourself out of the memory by focusing on your feet. This will help ground you. Look at the objects in your room and name them. "There's a table, and a lamp, a window, and a chair." Remind yourself that you're an adult now who is safe and protected. Get up and walk around to reorient yourself to the here and now. You can look at your surroundings and tell yourself, "I'm in my adult home now, where I'm safe." Being swept up in a scene from the past can happen, and it's nothing to feel ashamed of. But it's better to stop the encounter until you can be a *witness* rather than an overwhelmed participant. Feeling lost and frightened in a scene from your past *won't* be a healing experience. It can even be re-traumatizing. If this continues to happen to you, because it is not healing, it is wise to access your inner parts with a therapist present.

As adults, when we give words to our early, even pre-verbal shame experiences, we are bringing an adult's perspective. Ideally, this perspective allows us to reevaluate our all-encompassing negative feelings toward ourselves and our parts. For example, we may see that we aren't "all bad," but, instead, hurt and scared. Even if we become aware of things we did—transgressions, mistakes, hurtful behavior—we can see that those behaviors don't warrant global feelings of worthlessness. Those mistakes were our *behaviors*, the *behaviors* of our parts lost in the past—not who we were or are. Those mistakes were the actions that reflect what it means to be lost and confused without guidance and support—they are not evidence of being broken or worthless.

As you continue to work with your inner selves—listening to them with compassion and clarifying false beliefs they may have about themselves—eventually, not only will the scenes recede into the past, but best of all, the feelings these parts hold of not mattering, not being good enough, or being broken, angry, or dirty will also begin to fade. But bear in mind: this requires a purposeful intention to know that when you feel distressed—whether anxious, depressed, scared, angry, or distrustful, to name a few—a part has likely been triggered. It's your job to be a healing, good parent and to check in with your inner parts: "What's up? What do you want me to know?" Strive always to be curious rather than critical of your parts. If it is not convenient for you to work with a part when it's triggered, talk to them as you would talk to a child: "I can't talk with you right this minute, but I will talk with you later when it's quiet and I can focus on what you want me to share with me. For now, can you just watch and let me finish this task? When we're home, we can talk." Then, be absolutely certain that you keep your word and make time for them.

Remember that all parts exist because they have unhealed emotional burdens, and to heal, they need your attention and compassionate understanding toward whatever they experienced.

Thank them for being there for you. They took the abuse, neglect, and mistreatment. Be grateful for this amazing psychological phenomenon, regardless of whether you believe in or understand it—it was your mind's way of keeping your sanity. Now, thankfully, you can use your adult perspective and your mature feelings of compassion and understanding to give your burdened, unhealed parts the healing they deserve.

For further guidance, Richard Schwartz's recent book, *No Bad Parts* (Schwartz 2021), is an excellent comprehensive guide with specific exercises. For self-paced work with your parts, check out Jay Earley's book, *Self-Therapy: A Step-By-Step Guide to Creating Wholeness and Healing Your Inner Child Using IFS, a New Cutting-Edge Psychotherapy* (J. Earley 2009). This too is a very comprehensive book with illustrations, session dialogues, and explanations of the functions our parts had in our past. But if doing this alone frightens you in any way, seek the help of a trusted friend or trained therapist.

As parts are re-membered into your conscious awareness and their traumas are healed, these parts will fade into the background of your past. Still, they will leave their talents and energies as gifts to use in your life.

Chapter Takeaways

1. The process of engaging in healing dialogues with our inner parts can be a powerful tool for personal growth and emotional healing. It must never be re-traumatizing.

2. If your trauma is ongoing and you have feelings, thoughts, or dreams of hurting yourself or someone else, or if your thoughts or feelings scare you, DO NOT engage in this process without a professional.

3. When initiating these dialogues, it's crucial to approach our inner parts with gentleness and curiosity, much as we would with a child or a teenager. Building trust is key.

4. The primary goal of these encounters is to unburden the young parts that carry pain, feelings, and beliefs from the past. Similar to how children are unburdened by sharing their experiences with adults, our inner parts benefit from having their stories heard without judgment and with genuine compassion.

5. Sometimes, we may encounter angry or challenging inner parts, which may actually be protectors of younger, wounded parts. Recognizing their role in keeping us safe, even if it seems counterproductive, can soften our feelings toward them and help us appreciate their efforts.

Reflection Question

Reflect on a recent instance where you felt anxious, depressed, scared, angry, or distrustful. If you considered that these feelings are a message from an inner part, how might you approach them with curiosity rather than skepticism or judgment?

Practice

This practice draws from the last three chapters and should only be undertaken if you feel comfortable and safe with it.

1.   Begin by taking a few moments to focus on your breath and relax. Close your eyes if it helps you to center yourself.

2.   Reflect on a specific emotion, sensation, or memory that you've been struggling with or that feels particularly significant at this moment. It could be a feeling of fear, sadness, anger, or any other emotion.

3.   Inwardly address this emotion or sensation by saying something like "Whose feelings are these? I want to meet you" or "Who is feeling [insert emotion]? Will you talk to me?"

4.   The memory could be a snippet or a full sequence. Try to discern what is happening in the memory. Who are the characters? Are any of them you or a younger version of you?

5.   Inwardly address this person or younger you as you would address a young friend. "Hi, I'd like to meet you. I'd like to just hang out here for a minute. Would that be okay?"

6.   Be patient and open to whatever arises within you. You might receive an image, a feeling, or even a vague sense of a presence. This is your inner part responding.

7.   Engage your inner part gently and compassionately. Ask nonintrusive questions, just as you would with a child or a vulnerable person. For example:

- "How old are you?"
- "What made you feel this way?"
- "Is there anything you want to share with me?"
- "What do you need from me to feel safe?"

8. Listen attentively to the responses you receive. Validate the feelings and experiences without judgment.

9. After you have listened to all they want to share and you have validated their feelings, thank your inner part for opening up and sharing with you. Express gratitude for their presence and the opportunity to meet them.

10. If you encounter resistance or feel overwhelmed during the dialogue, practice grounding techniques like focusing on your breath or visualizing your feet on solid ground. Remind yourself that you are safe in the present moment. It's critical that you are grounded and not caught up in the scene.

11. Consider writing about your experience in your notebook. Reflect on any insights, emotions, or revelations that emerged during the conversation with your inner part.

12. As you continue to work on healing your inner parts, make a commitment to check in with them whenever you experience distressing emotions or triggers. Be curious, not critical, and provide them with the understanding and compassion they need.

13. Continue to write in your notebook about your experiences. You will read them again one day and be amazed at how healing your work has been.

11

Habits That Feed Shame and Delay Healing

Repeated thoughts become a habit. A repeated habit becomes a belief. Believing we are not good enough and unworthy is a habitual thought that has become a belief and something we can change.

—Unknown

Our shame wounding happened in the past, but often-times, we unknowingly keep these wounds open and oozing. Our past experiences hurt us, but what if we continue to feel badly not because of what happened to us, but by how we are keeping them alive. I know this is a bold statement, but how could we not continue to feel terrible when we carry and repeat the very demeaning and false beliefs that our perpetrators and unconscious parents told us? So the question is, what are we doing that blocks our healing and keeps our pain alive? Here are a few possibilities:

1. Habitually repeating shame-speak.
2. Believing and not challenging the belief that we are broken, unworthy, unlovable.
3. Mindlessly retelling of our childhood trauma stories.
4. Keeping company with those who reinforce our negative views of ourselves.
5. Accepting that we must be perfect in order to be loved.
6. Practicing poor self-care, which includes comparing ourselves to others, watching bummer TV, and participating in negative social media.

We have already discussed how shame-speak is the put-down and judging chatter in our heads, but now we need to learn how to confront it.

Mindlessly repeating shame-speak hurts and re-wounds us. *Our minds and bodies don't distinguish between what someone says to us and what we say to ourselves.* Therefore, when we mindlessly tell ourselves, "you're such a loser," our minds and bodies react as though it is the truth. The wounding inflicted by these mindless phrases is so lacerating that it's like severing an emotional artery. We must do everything possible to stop the bleeding. No one can do it for us. It's up to us, and, fortunately, we have the power to prevent this self-betrayal.

More about shame-speak

Your first step in stopping shame-speak is noticing when these words come out of your mouth or enter your *thoughts*. This means you become as vigilant about your shame-speak as you are about who you let into your home. You wouldn't let someone who belittled and hurt you into your home, and shame-speak is like hanging out with an attacker. You must label it as an unacceptable intruder in your home, heart, and mind. "This is shame-speak," you must say to yourself, "and this is interfering with my healing. I'm *not* going to keep working for shame. I will stop repeating shame-speak, even if a part of me thinks the harsh judgment is correct."

Even when you're vigilant, shame-speak doesn't stop immediately. These are old thought habits, and the words and beliefs will continue to creep into your mind. But labeling them as false beliefs and stopping yourself from saying them aloud or just in your mind will give you more power to change or eliminate them.

Shame-speak may have served a purpose in your past. When you were young and traumatized to the point of sub-mit–appease–collapse, your nervous system chose to respond by diminishing yourself to appease someone stronger and more powerful than you were. Shame-speak functioned to accomplish that. It told you to go small, to appease and submit. But you no longer need to keep yourself small and non-threatening to an aggressor. Quite the opposite!

Over time, shame-speak becomes a habit like biting your fingernails when you're anxious. You can theorize about why you do it, but even if you come up with a plausible reason, you still must decide that you don't want to do it anymore and stop. The same is true about shame-speak. It will not happen on its own. When you consistently stop the shame-speak—and only then—you'll notice that shame-thoughts and the habit of shame-speak will show up less and less. But you must stay vigilant and committed to ending this debili-tating habit or it will creep back in.

Changing our shame-speak beliefs

Our shame-speak is a window into what we believe is true about us. Many of us have tried countering our shame-speak with facts. For example, have you attempted to undo "I am stupid" by pointing to your accomplishments or education? Did you notice, as I did, that this didn't make much of a dent? There are several reasons why: facts, data points, lists of accomplishments, titles, skills, degrees, and promotions are the content of the left brain, which is the logical part of our brain. Our shame injuries live in our right brain, which is the emotional part of our brain. Therefore, left-brain thinking (data-based) alone doesn't undo or heal emotional wounds. But when the logical and emotional sides of the brain work together, they can correct them. When we heal our "parts" that carry shame-beliefs, the source of our shame-speak, it is almost entirely a process of emotional healing.

A healing sequence goes like this. We can ask ourselves, "Is it true that I am stupid?" Our left brain then provides the data. The question "How did I come to think of myself that way?" activates the right brain, and we may remember experiences of someone hurling that label at us. Those were painful moments, and for several reasons (such as, they were authority figures; they were stronger and might punish us if we disagreed; or we really had no way of knowing if they were correct), we accepted the accusation as true. But now we can make a different choice. Ask yourself again, "Was it true?"

Children naturally make mistakes, and every mistake is a learning opportunity. When kids make mistakes and then hear "that was stupid" or "how can you be so stupid?" they are being told that making mistakes is evidence of stupidity.

This is not true. The worst of it is that this kind of accusation becomes part of the child's sense of self.

In addition, we all have different intellectual strengths, and sometimes these differences can be used against us. For example, my stepfather was very good at retaining facts. I am a big-picture thinker, and facts or details often escape me. So, when he would initiate a conversation, which was always a debate, I would inevitably fall short of facts, and he would emerge looking smarter while I always seemed dumber.

As we try to sort out the facts, the next step in the healing sequence involves the left brain. Now I have the data that I'm not stupid and I have the insight that my stepfather, who tried to finish his engineering degree and dropped out, may have felt stupid and projected it onto me. (Remember that projection is when someone unconsciously takes unwanted emotions or traits they don't like about themselves and attributes them to someone else.) Now I can tell myself, "This label does not belong to me. It is not true that I am stupid. That label is not mine." When we emphasize that "stupid" is not about us with the same confidence we'd generate if someone falsely accused us of stealing their dog, both the left and the right brain are working together. How many times do we need to repeat "It is not mine!" to pull this fishhook out of our psyche? This falsehood! As many as it takes, even a hundred times a day. Training your brain to challenge false negative beliefs—to let them go, to dismiss them, instead of accepting them as true—takes practice. This is the practice of self-appreciation and self-care.

For us as adults, it helps to use our logical minds to understand the origins and the inaccuracies of our shame-speak. For example, consider the common shame-speak phrase,

"I'm not good enough." When we become aware of such thoughts or feelings, we can ask ourselves, "Not good enough for what?" Maybe we felt not good enough to be accepted and loved by our mother, father, or caretaker. As a child, we couldn't make sense of our parents' feelings toward us other than to conclude that it must be something about us. Young children lack the perspective of sorting out what's them and what's someone else. Remember that children will choose to think there's something wrong with them rather than believe they're alone without protective, loving parents in a dangerous world.

Perhaps "stupid" or "not good enough" isn't your most frequent shame-speak. What is? "Ugly ... fat ... crazy ... broken ... worthless"? Remember that the first step is to decide to stop repeating these phrases and words to yourself even if a part of you believes it is true. Vow to stop the bleeding, and as you do, you'll be amazed at the difference. Remember too that those words and the feelings that accompany them are false labels that someone projected on you. Most likely, one of your caretakers felt those awful things were true about themself.

What will you experience when the shame-speak recedes? It will feel as though a mugger who has attacked you for as long as you can remember has backed off. You'll have fewer anxious thoughts and fewer physical feelings of endangerment. Will it happen overnight? Probably not, but someday, when you have also healed the part or parts that carry those beliefs, you'll reflect back and notice that the chronic inner turmoil has quieted. Believe me—you'll be forever grateful. Still, when you're threatened or under a lot of stress, those shame-speak phrases may make another appearance. But now you know how to work with shame-speak, and combined with the antidotes you'll learn in the following chapters, you can disentangle yourself from them and return to your newfound self. That's how it has been for me and many of my clients.

The poison of comparing yourself to others

All of us compare ourselves to—well, you name it. We're socialized to compare ourselves from a very early age. This is a socially sanctioned form of judgment, and social media has dramatically increased this toxin. Shame is the only negative emotion of self-judgment we use to turn against ourselves to keep ourselves small and non-threatening to our aggressor. But now the aggressor is you. Can you see why unfavorable comparisons and judgments make us fearful and self-loath-ing? Again, when we do this, we've clocked-in and we work for shame.

What can we do about this socially sanctioned, shame-driven habit of comparing ourselves to others? The answer is simple but challenging. Comparing ourselves and coming out either *better* or *less than* is self-shaming, so it's import-ant to limit the time you indulge in this destructive habit. Aim for zero time. Staying away from social media sites, people, or situations that increase the probability of misery from self-judgment is key. Many a client has resisted my sugges-tions that they limit social media time or turn off the news that upsets them. They protest, saying they are afraid they will miss something. I agree. They will miss the misery these sources inflict on their sense of well-being and compassion.

Belief in the power of perfection

Another poison is the need to be perfect. Since children believe their imperfections cause their parents' mistreatment, it's easy for them to think they can win their parents' love by becoming perfect. Children learn early that if they want to keep the fragile connection they have with their significant others, they must attend to the messages of how the parent wants them to be: get the best grades, look beautiful, be smart and social, win trophies, cheer the parent up, make the parent look good ... As children focus on these cues, they must learn to mute their own emerging needs. They cannot afford to follow their own cues, their own callings. Over time, they become emptier, more confused, more compliant and accommodating—more shame filled.

Often children and adults find it difficult to accept that their parents didn't know how to love them, and it had nothing to do with the child's behaviors or performance—nothing to do with being the best or making mommy proud. This misperception that perfection in terms of meeting the needs and expectations of another person brings love is something akin to the belief that being good brings Santa and gifts. It is at the root of so much unnecessary suffering.

Do you link being loved with needing to be perfect or perceived as perfect? Have you ever thought, "Wait until they find out who I really am!" Some call this the imposter syndrome, but it's all shame at its core. We can't ensure that adults in our life will love and accept us if we're thin, beautiful, smart, or clever. Instead, we need to find those who know how to love and invite them into our lives.

There are other things that keep our shame wounds bleeding. I'll introduce these with a story from my own life.

Sharing our shame stories

As a young adult, I had plenty of shame stories. I often told them to friends without ever considering that there could be a downside. I had my favorite stories and was very good at telling them. Usually, this led to someone telling a story about their own mistreatment, and I would feel less alone. Others had suffered too, and while many had suffered more, I felt validated in that I'd been mistreated and that the pain and anger I felt were legitimate.

But one day, after I finished one of my favorite stories, a friend and colleague said, "Kristine, where is the news?" I was shocked.

News? This wasn't supposed to be news. Then I thought, *don't you care about me? This is who I am.*

I was astonished that I had those thoughts. It shocked me to realize that I had become so identified with my suffering that my yardstick for whether my friends cared about me was their willingness to listen to my stories.

But these stories had other purposes as well. When I told my stories, I felt the energy of indignation and anger. I was back in the scene, both as an adult and as a younger self, and often I was feeling the strength of anger as well as the shame of those experiences. These feelings had a power to them that I liked. I also wanted sympathy. Maybe that's not all bad, but what price did I pay for those moments? Without realizing it, I was reliving and keeping those memories and feelings—anger, humiliation, shame, and outrage—alive.

They weren't in the past for me because I was still feeling them and unknowingly feeding them. I was working for shame.

I mistakenly thought my healing would come primarily from outside of me—from the validation and sympathy from others. I thought if I told these stories of how awful my stepfather was or how emotionally rejecting and passive my mother was, eventually someone or enough people would say something to me enough times, and bingo! I'd be over it. I carried the fantasy that my self-confidence would be fixed, my low self-esteem would soar into the normal zone, and I'd feel worthy of love. I was wrong. Healing is an inside job. Others assist and can be instrumental, but, in the end, it all happens inside us by our own efforts.

There is another reason we tell our stories. It's probably a motivation you'll recognize. *We want to hurt those who hurt us.* We don't want them to get away with how cruel or awful they were. We want others to know their dark side, not to let them hide behind their public persona of being a good and caring person. We want them to hurt as we were hurt. But is that possible? Can you ever make your offender hurt like you did as a child? As adults can they ever feel as lost in the maze of shame, confusion, and fear as what you experienced? Could they ever feel as unworthy or defective as you did? No! Never! We can't make an adult offender hurt as we did as a child.

So, this is the question: Do you want to spend your life energy pursuing vengeance, especially a revenge that will never be fulfilled? I assure you that doing so requires you to constantly live in a past I'm confident you'd rather leave behind.

Brene Brown advocated "If *we* can *share our story* with someone who responds with empathy and understanding, shame can't survive." (Brown). How is the sharing Brown describes different from telling and retelling our stories in an unhealthy way? If we have shared our stories and received kindness and support but find ourselves drawn to repeating them over and over, we must ask ourselves about our motivation. For example, I recently attended a small group organized by a local health practitioner. As we introduced ourselves, one woman in the group told us her name and quickly added, "I'm an incest survivor." What was her motivation? Had this become her identity? By sharing that she was an incest survivor, was she dispelling shame? We won't know her intentions, but we need to be careful not to fall into the painful trap of making our wounding our identity. We are all more than anything that ever happened to us.

The next time you find yourself wanting to share a story of mistreatment or abuse, ask yourself, what is my motivation? What are you needing? What does the part of you that carries that experience need? What you want and need may be healthy, but you must also be careful. By sharing your story of abuse, for example, are you limiting how others see you and you see yourself? Are you keeping the past alive when it needs to be healed so it can recede into the past?

If validation and sympathy from others won't heal us and getting revenge won't either, what are we to do with all these awful feelings we have? First, we must learn to take care of those feelings in a way that helps us heal from the inside. Let's explore how we can do that in the next chapter.

———•———

Chapter Takeaways

1. It's crucial to become aware of the shame-speak that occurs in your thoughts or speech and refuse to repeat them.

2. Simply countering shame-speak with facts and logic is not enough to heal emotional wounds. Emotional processing and self-compassion—not just intellectual arguments against negative beliefs—are key.

3. The pursuit of perfection to gain love or acceptance is a harmful belief. It never works. Seek relationships with those who genuinely know how to love and will accept you for who you are, imperfections and all.

4. Constantly comparing yourself to others feeds self-judgment and self-loathing. Try to limit activities or situations that encourage unfavorable comparisons. Use your time and energy to focus on what you like about yourself.

5. Be mindful of how you share your past experiences of mistreatment or abuse. Avoid turning your wounds into your identity or telling your stories as a way to seek revenge on those who hurt you. Always consider the motivation behind sharing these stories and whether it contributes to your healing.

Reflection Question

There are two emotions that comment on the self. Shame is always negative and demeaning. The other? Pride. Feeling proud or pride is the opposite of shame. What are three things about yourself that you feel proud of?

Practice

Think of a time when you shared a shame story. Ask yourself the following questions:

- "What did I hope to achieve by sharing my shame story?"
- "How does it feel when I share these stories?"
- "Am I keeping the past alive instead of allowing it to heal? Why?"
- "Have there been times when I stopped myself from sharing a shame story because I could see it wasn't helpful to my healing?" If so, good for you!

12

Soothing as an Antidote to Shame's Wounding

We get our first lessons in self-care from the way we were cared for. Children whose parents were reliable sources of comfort and strength have a lifetime advantage—a kind of buffer against the worst that fate can hand them.

—Bessel van der Kolk

My client, Diana, recounted a time when her father told her he was worried they would lose their house because he didn't have money to pay the mortgage. She was five years old, and it scared her. "You can have the money in my piggy bank," she told him.

Her dad responded, "Well, it hasn't come to that yet, but if it does, your piggy bank money will certainly help."

"Well," she said, comforting him, "no matter what, we'll still have our mattresses."

Sometimes, overwhelmed parents don't protect their children from adult worries. Worse still is when children are afraid and the adult offers no comfort. Diana had to comfort her father *and* her five-year-old self. She had grown up in a family of chaos and neglect, and now she was comforting her father! Diana reminded me of other clients—tough on the outside but struggling and deprived on the inside. I'm reminded of a get-well card a friend sent me. On the front was the back view of a zebra flat on its back, feet in the air. The caption, "No, no. I'm fine. Just give me a minute." Many of us learned to take care of ourselves because no one was there for us.

To be truly strong and resilient from the *inside,* children need years of comfort and soothing from their parents. Knowing how to soothe yourself is one of the greatest gifts of being raised by safe and attuned caretakers. "Soothing is one of the kindest gestures that humans ever perform for one another." (*The School of Life* 2019) Later, when emotional storms hit, when you are panicking and fear that you will die, when your heart feels broken and you believe you are totally alone, you remember how your parents' comforting words could work magic for you. You feel less afraid knowing you have been through these wild seas before and you always lived to see the sun again. You are able to conjure up their words and hear one part of your mind comforting the other part.

Fortunately, if you did not have parents who reliably comforted you, you can learn to do this for yourself as an adult.

Were you adequately soothed?

Take a moment to remember back to your childhood. Do you remember early life experiences of being held and comforted? For example, do you remember a safe adult comforting you at age five or eight? Were you comforted when you fell off your bike and skinned your knees or fell out of a tree and broke your arm? How about at age ten or twelve? You'll know the answers to these questions by looking within. Are there calming words or feelings that immediately spring to mind when you're upset? Do phrases like, "You're going to be okay," "You can get help," "Someone will help you figure this out," "Everyone makes mistakes," or "It's okay" spring quickly to mind when you're upset?

Sadly, for many of us, the answer is "no." Too many of us were raised by parents who couldn't give us this invaluable inheritance. Even if we have calm, supportive people in our lives today, we still need to learn and cultivate our self-soothing abilities intentionally. As adults, learning what soothes us is one of the most critical skills we must develop. Let me emphasize this. When you learn how to soothe yourself, your life and relationships will be easier.

But we need to develop these abilities when we're in a calm state because during our emotional storms, our survival brain shuts down our logical brain, and we are thrown into the fight-flight-freeze or appease responses. As a result, we literally can't think logically. But suppose we have access to self-soothing strategies so that when the storm overtakes us, we have the skills to avoid the horrible out-of-control feeling. To do this, we need a well-practiced, easy remedy that we don't have to think about. Otherwise, desperate people do desperate things. Luckily, we can learn what soothes us.

For example, Charlotte went to a retirement party for a friend, where she ran into a couple she hadn't seen in years. As she greeted them, she sensed how distant and cold they were. Puzzled, she remembered the last time she had seen them and realized it was at a party where she got drunk and became emotionally unmoored. The combination of that shameful memory and the couple's coldness was too much, so Charlotte left the party early. On the way home, she tried to call her girlfriend. No answer. She arrived home and called her sister. No answer. So, she told me, she began comforting herself. "What did you say?" I asked her.

"I told myself what I wanted to hear," she said. "I validated my own feelings. No one deserves to be treated so rudely, no matter what they've done. I said some other nice things to myself about how I don't drink like that anymore and I can calm myself down when I'm upset. And I don't have those meltdowns anymore. I'm so proud of myself. Those tools we've worked on—they work. I can calm myself. I know how to do that now, and although I want comfort from my friends when I'm upset, if they're not available, I can do it myself."

Charlotte had worked hard to develop this ability to self-soothe. She had taken the support from our work together and overridden her inner shame-speak messages that said she didn't deserve to feel good about herself. I was so happy for her, I cheered!

We have all tried to find things that soothe us, but when we do not have a clear sense of what works, we turn to actions that may be temporarily soothing like drugs, drinking, video gaming, or sex. Sadly, these eventually make us feel more miserable. In desperation, some people try cutting themselves, starving, bulimia, or over-exercising. These all work temporarily, but they're dangerous, as you know, and ultimately leave us feeling more broken. We do these things not because we are bad, stupid, or damaged. We tried these things because we didn't know how to soothe ourselves in a healthy way. No one else adequately soothed us, so we didn't have the modeling or internal resources to soothe ourselves.

Like Charlotte, however, we don't have to be at the mercy of our emotional storms. With time, commitment, and practice, we can become proficient self-soothers. This seemingly small accomplishment is just as significant as learning to walk.

Processes for becoming a self-soother

By learning to self-soothe, we can create a reservoir of comforting words, feelings, and actions. We can build this essential skill for ourselves even though our parents couldn't adequately do so. Here are a few processes you can use to self-soothe. You may have some to add to this list.

Breathing

Breathing is how we regulate our physiology, stress hormones, and, therefore, our emotions. Consider these common phrases: "We held our breath in anticipation," "I was so scared I couldn't breathe," and "He heaved a sigh of relief." If this breathe-in and breathe-out rhythm is out of sync, it leaves us vulnerable to quickly becoming upset and overreacting to disappointments and frustrations. Research has confirmed that changing the way we breathe can improve problems with anger, depression, and anxiety.

There are many different forms and ways to practice focused breathing or meditation. But all beginning meditators find that as they tune inward and listen in on their minds, their thoughts are like a bunch of two-year-olds racing around, undisciplined and into everything. This inner chaos can be disconcerting and often leads people to believe they can't meditate. But that's just how the unmanaged mind is. Our thoughts race off into the future, worrying about an upcoming meeting, or they go back into the past to rehash a conversation or relive a sad and painful memory.

Without having practiced managing your mind, you're almost always either in the past or the future. Many meditation practices point out that staying in the present is where the peace and calm we seek await us. Meditation has been shown by years of solid research to be physically and emotionally beneficial.

Focused attention and loving kindness

These are two popular forms of meditation: focused attention and loving kindness. Focused attention meditation involves focusing on an object. It can be a candle, flower, or simply (my favorite) the rise and fall of your breath. As you practice focusing on whatever you've chosen, you'll notice that your mind takes off and becomes engaged in all sorts of stories. When you observe this, patiently and kindly return your focus to the object. Practicing this for ten to fifteen minutes a day is enough to be beneficial.

Here are the steps:

1. Find a quiet place where you won't be interrupted, such as in the car, in the bathroom, in a park, or in your bedroom.
2. Sit in a comfortable position.

3. Close your eyes, relax, and focus on your breath—the sound, the sensation in your nostrils, or the rising and falling of your chest.
4. Slowly draw in your breath and then enjoy the sensation of release. Repeat.
5. As your mind wanders, gently bring it back to your focus—your breath.
6. Your mind will naturally become engaged in another thought or worry.
7. Try to release the thought and focus back on your breath.
8. You can count your breaths if that helps you focus.
9. You may experience twitches, itches, and yawns. It's all normal.
10. Continue for fifteen minutes. Start with less time if needs be.

Fifteen minutes of focused meditation a day for a month has been shown to lift your mood, clear your mind, and make you more sensitive to the promptings of your inner being. It also allows you to disengage from negative thoughts more easily.

Loving-kindness meditation is an ancient practice in which you purposefully send loving, kind thoughts and emotions to yourself and all living beings by repeating a set of statements. The instruction for this practice is to begin by saying the phrases (see below) and sending loving messages to yourself. Then, repeat the words while thinking of someone you love and care about. Next, focus on someone you feel neutral about and then someone you feel negative toward.

Finally, say the meditation phrases with all of humanity in your mind. Here is a set of loving-kindness statements:

> May I be happy (May you be happy).
> May I (you) be peaceful.
> May I (you) be well.
> May I (you) live with ease.
> May I (you) find deep joy.
> May I (you) be free of pain.
> May I (you) be free from harm.
> May I (you) be free of suffering.
> May I (you) feel safe.

When your attention wanders, as it will, kindly return your thoughts to sending love and caring. If you'd like to be guided during your meditation, there are many guided meditations by a pioneer in this form of meditation, Tara Brach. (Brach n.d.) Also, see the resources section at the back of this book.

Andrew Villamil, a graduate student and researcher on the benefits of meditation, has said this about loving-kindness meditation: "When kind intention is practiced, individuals are able to build prosocial behavior through empathy, compassion, and kindness. This practice recruits areas of the brain that maintain health and support individual well-being, while simultaneously providing support toward the well-being of "others and all living beings." (Villamil, et al. 2019)

How does spending time in meditation contribute to self-soothing? Villamil also says, "Most research shows that, if practiced daily, an individual can begin to alter neural (brain) connections within eight weeks, creating a mental state of well-being that is primed to become a long term, altered trait. In this way, the active state created in a practice becomes a positive shift in state that will then become generalized and engaged throughout non-practice times." In other words, daily meditation alters our brains even when we aren't actively meditating, and those positive gains stay with us.

Hand on heart

Do you know about the calming effect of putting your hand on your heart area and breathing through your hand? Try it. Placing your hand on your heart is more than just a friendly gesture—I've discovered that there's a science to this. The research of a respected organization called HeartMath includes twenty-five years of studies that help us understand our heart's relationship to our brain and emotions.

The research of Childre and Martin at the HeartMath Institute has shown that contrary to what we generally think, our brain *is not* the boss of our body and feelings. Instead, it is our *heart*. We generally think of our heart as a faithful puppy, dutifully pumping along and following the Big Dog Brain. But we're wrong. HeartMath's researchers have shown that the heart sends thousands more messages to the brain than the brain sends to the heart. Imagine that! Research has also shown that the heart has its own independent complex nervous system called "the brain in the heart." Our heart is not just a little pumper. Instead, it significantly influences the brain and the brain's emotional processing— every heartbeat of our lives.

HeartMath research shows that we can increase the heart's calming effect on our brains and bodies by intentionally recalling times when we felt appreciation, gratitude, or joy. Sitting quietly and thinking of something that delights you or that you appreciate is all it takes. When I first learned about this, I had a new puppy, Zoey, and her antics delighted me. All I had to do was think about her, and I was flooded with joy and gratitude. I also practiced remembering things and people I was grateful for, a process my grandmother called "counting our blessings." The research proves that when we feel gratitude, caring, and love, our brain and heart get into a synchronized rhythm that calms and soothes us. Because the brain-in-the-heart influences the brain's processing of our emotions, it enhances our thinking function, creativity, and resiliency. The heart is where the gifts of the spirit are activated, and today, we need the love of our own hearts more than ever.

This is compelling stuff. And I think it points to our heart as the seat of healing, something the ancients discovered eons ago. If you'd like to know more, check out www.heartmath.com.

Physical soothing

As infants, our soothing begins with the physical actions of our caretakers—rocking, cuddling, holding, bouncing, talking softly, and singing. These are our first experiences, and they're deeply embedded in our emotional brain and body. Many adults feel better with a safe, warm, and welcoming embrace from someone they trust. But when we're raised in an atmosphere of fear and lack of safety, we often don't trust anyone enough to find their embrace soothing. Hugs might scare us.

So how do you physically comfort yourself as an adult? Perhaps by having a warm shower, a bubble bath, or a soak with soothing bath salts. Maybe by listening to calming music. Do you have a favorite Pandora or Spotify channel that is your go-to for comfort? Do you like bundling up in a blanket or lying in the sun? Do you eat a favorite food? Physical comfort is so essential and fundamental. It's soothing to get into a curled-up position on your bed and pull the covers over you to make a warm, dark tent. It doesn't matter what you use for physical soothing. There's no wrong or right, as long as it doesn't involve self-harm, an eating disorder, or addiction.

The power of music

We have all felt our mood shift as we listened to a familiar song from our youth. Listening, we are transported back to the time when that song had a powerful meaning in our lives. Even music we may not be familiar with has the power to move us. Parents and caretakers sing to their infants to comfort and soothe them. Sad, hopeful, melancholy, uplifting—music has been called a great healer, even reflective of the divine.

Research has shown that music significantly impacts neurochemical responses in the brain, particularly dopamine and endorphins. Dopamine is a neurotransmitter that is associated with pleasure and reward, and endorphins are natural painkillers released during exercise and other activities. Listening to music has been shown to raise dopamine levels by nine percent. Studies show that when you listen to music, your brain releases both chemicals, which can help to improve your mood and reduce feelings of anxiety and depression. One study found that listening to music for just thirty minutes a day for two weeks can lead to significant reductions in symptoms of depression and anxiety.

The power of music is its ability to stimulate our brains on multiple levels. Music can help us access insight into our inner worlds while helping us build resilience against life's challenges. There's no doubt that music plays an essential role in providing comfort during times of distress.

Create your own personal playlist. There is no magic genre of music. Any music can be used as long as it resonates and has a strong emotional connection with you. Spend some time reflecting on what music moves you; make a list of tunes that soothe and comfort, uplift, and inspire. The key is to remember to turn to this music and let yourself be absorbed into its power to change you.

The love of pets

If you have a pet, you know how much comfort they can bring as you play or snuggle beside them. You may not realize it, but the time you spend loving and playing with your pet is time invested in helping you heal. In an experiment by HeartMath, a boy and his pet dog were wired to record their heart rhythms. The boy entered the room and sat on the floor where his pet was waiting. He didn't touch or relate to his dog, Mabel, other than to consciously beam love toward her. Almost immediately, both the dog's and boy's heart rhythms came into sync with each other. When the boy left the room, both experienced a heart rhythm characteristic of distress. (McCarty 2001)

To enhance your self-soothing time with your pet, focus on your heart and let yourself feel the love you have for them. Notice the warm feelings. Do you know that *sending* love to your pet allows your heart to feel love? This means you don't have to wait for someone to love you to feel love. But you don't even need a pet to feel love. Every time you beam love out to someone—even a stranger in the grocery store or a child in a car next to you—you're experiencing love. And we can all use more love.

Gratitude

We may not think gratitude is a soothing process, but research shows it differently. In the last decade, multiple studies have shown gratitude enhances emotional well-being. In one study, 300 college students who sought counseling for depression and anxiety were randomly divided into three groups. Although all three groups received counseling services, the first group was also instructed to write one letter of gratitude to someone each week for three weeks. (The letters did not have to be mailed, and many weren't.) The second group was asked to write about their deepest thoughts and feelings about negative experiences, and the third group did not do any writing activity. All received counseling.

What did the researchers find? The participants who wrote about negative experiences and those who only received counseling did not fare as well as those who wrote gratitude letters. The letter writers reported better mental health at four weeks and twelve weeks after their writing exercise ended. "This suggests that gratitude writing can be beneficial for those who struggle with mental health concerns. In fact, it seems, practicing gratitude on top of receiving psychological counseling carries greater benefits than counseling alone, even when that gratitude practice is brief." (Brown, J. Wong, J. 2017)

Why is letter writing or gratitude journal keeping beneficial? Perhaps it concerns the emotions the writer feels as they write. Gratitude helps unshackle us from toxic emotions because the writer is magnifying the experience of positive emotions. They feel the positive effect of the words and thoughts they write. Brain imaging supports the writers' self-reporting of feeling happier and less anxious. Images of the writers' brains showed greater activation in the medial prefrontal cortex, which regulates anxiety, emotional-social behavior, motivation, cognition, sociability, and feelings of affiliation.

"This is striking as this effect was found three months after the letter writing ended. This indicates that simply expressing gratitude may have lasting effects on the brain. While not conclusive, this finding suggests that practicing gratitude may help train the brain to be more sensitive to the experience of gratitude down the line, and this could contribute to improved mental health over time." (Brown, J. Wong, J. 2017)

While there are many suggestions for journaling, Robert Emmons, a professor at the University of California, Davis, arguably the world's leading expert on the science of gratitude and an author of some of the seminal studies of gratitude journals, provides further guidance on journaling. He has studied over one thousand people aged eight to eighty.

"Don't overdo it," Emmons suggests. Writing occasionally (once or twice weekly) is more beneficial than daily journaling. One study found that people who wrote in their gratitude journals once a week for six weeks reported boosts in happiness afterward. Surprisingly, those who wrote three times per week did not. "We adapt to positive events quickly, especially if we constantly focus on them," says Emmons. "It seems counter-intuitive, but it is how the mind works." (Emmons 2010)

According to a study that Emmons references, the most essential component of beneficial journaling is making a decision that you want to feel happier and more grateful. Do not just go through the motions. Being specific about what you are grateful for is more effective at eliciting the benefits of gratitude than just making a list. Example: I am grateful for the ride my friend James gave me to the airport on Thursday. "Focusing on people to whom you are grateful has more of an impact than focusing on things for which you are grateful." (Emmons 2010)

Savor surprises, Emmons suggests. "Try to record events that were unexpected or surprising, as these tend to elicit stronger levels of gratitude." (Emmons 2010) This may surprise you but writing occasionally (once or twice per week) was found to be more beneficial than daily journaling. "We adapt to positive events quickly, especially if we constantly focus on them," says Emmons. (Marsh 2011) This is not to discount daily journaling if that is what you prefer, especially if you do it for a specific time period.

Unlike just thinking about what we're grateful for, journaling promotes a greater depth of feeling. Translating thoughts and feelings into words helps deepen the experience. If we also look at each event or person for which we feel gratitude as a gift, we become more aware of our feelings and can "relish" and "savor" this gift in our imagination. "Take the time to be especially aware of the depth of your gratitude," Emmons wisely advises. Feeling gratitude toward others has been found to "reduce episodes of depression, increase a sense of self-worth, and make us more stress resistant. As we experience and savor the kindness of others, we feel less alone." (Emmons 2010) Experiencing and focusing on the caring others have shown us is soothing.

Nature

Intuitively, we've always known that being in nature, whether it's a forest, our garden, a park, or the ocean, can help us feel better. Sometimes it's difficult, even impossible, to feel fully present when we're there, however. Our mind is occupied with worries and incoming texts on our phones. So how can we soothe ourselves in such places if we aren't even present? Of course, we can leave our phones at home, but what about the mind? How do we get our minds to move away from the future or stop rehashing the past?

Recently, a friend introduced me to the Japanese art of shinrin-yoku, or "forest bathing." (Li 2018) This isn't bathing as we generally think, but rather an immersion in nature. It's an invitation to experience nature through our six senses. We slow down and savor the sounds, smells, and sights around us—perhaps touching the bark of a tree, smelling a wildflower, or watching a bird flit about for a few moments. This singular attention to nature is soothing. All of these intentional activities help bring us into the present moment, and the more we do them, the easier it is to return to that mind state. For example, the other day, I saw a giant, fat bumblebee go into the large yellow flower of my squash plant. He was in there so long that I thought he might have gotten stuck. But no, out he came and onto another flower. This little scene delighted me, and I had no other thoughts while I watched.

When was the last time you watched the clouds or smelled the earth? Did you know that trees and vegetation give off essential oils that benefit us? They calm our nervous systems and enhance our well-being. (Li 2018) Our time immersed in nature comforts us and helps us learn to soothe ourselves—we're in the lap of the Great Mother.

Your list at the ready

I've emphasized that knowing what soothes you is essential, but it must be available when you're too upset to remember what to do. So please make a list you can refer to and keep it in a convenient place. This ability to self-soothe was a birthright you didn't get enough of, and you need this skill as an antidote to life's pain and past wounds. In time, with practice, self-soothing will come to you naturally.

Self-soothing in action

One frosty winter night in the Sierra Mountains, I was returning home from walking my dog when I saw flames leaping out of my neighbor's chimney. At the same time, I saw my neighbor running out of the house, holding her toddler in her arms. Behind her was her eight-year-old daughter, Ashley, shoeless and half-asleep.

Safely out on the sidewalk, Ashley stood alone, crying, while her mother comforted her toddler. Seeing her distress, I put my arm around her. "Am I going to be okay?" she asked. "Yes," I told her. "Your dad has fire extinguishers, and the fire department is on its way."

She asked again, "Are we going to be okay?"

"Yes, yes," I told her. Then, as the flames jumped even higher, to my amazement, Ashley began to self-soothe.

"We're going to be okay," she said to herself. "It's only stuff. We have each other, and that's all that counts. We have nice neighbors who are our friends. We're going to be okay." Ashley had been given the gift of self-soothing.

This all seems simple enough, but we can never underestimate the power of self-soothing. How many times have you wanted to be calmer and more in control of your feelings, but didn't know how? Isn't this, in fact, one of your greatest desires? Did you know that people who suffer from mental health problems do so because of unmanaged, unregulated emotions? We all need to know how to self-soothe, and we can have these powerful resources available when we need them to lessen our suffering.

Chapter Takeaways

1. Children who have years of comfort and soothing from their parents develop inner resilience. This enables them to draw upon soothing words, feelings, and actions when facing difficulties throughout their lives.

2. If you were not adequately soothed in childhood, you will need to intentionally learn and cultivate self-soothing abilities. Possessing and using these skills is essential to becoming stress-resilient.

3. There are various techniques for self-soothing, including conscious breathing, mindfulness meditation, focusing on the heart, physical soothing, spending time with pets, gratitude journaling, and immersing oneself in nature. Creating a list of self-soothing strategies and keeping it readily available can help you manage your emotions effectively.

Reflection Question

Is music a soothing practice for you? What two songs are your favorite antidotes?

Practice

Self-soothing toolkit creation

1. Begin by setting aside some time to create your own self-soothing toolkit. This toolkit will serve as a collection of strategies and techniques that you can turn to when you need to self-soothe during challenging or distressing experiences.

2. Review the self-soothing techniques mentioned in the text, such as "Hand on Heart," "Loving-Kindness Meditation," "Focused Attention Meditation," "Gratitude Journaling," and "Nature Immersion." Choose practices that resonate with you but are not already part of your tool belt.

3. Commit to trying out your chosen self-soothing techniques regularly, especially when you're not in distress. This will help you become more familiar with them and make them more available and effective when you need them most.

4. Periodically revisit and update your self-soothing toolkit. As you discover new processes or find that some work better for you than others, add or subtract them. It's your toolkit.

13

The Healing Power of Self-Compassion and Self-Kindness

Because high-shame and self-critical people may have had little experience of compassion from others and from being self-compassionate, we have to teach it.

—Paul Gilbert

One spring afternoon, I came out of my house and saw my neighbor, Alexa, sitting on the ground, holding and talking to her adventurous seven-year-old son, Justin. He was sobbing and holding his ankle, and she was rocking him with her mouth up to his ear. I could hear her talking tenderly and compassionately. "I know it hurts. I know it hurts," I heard her say. "You're going to be okay. I'll take care of you." As his sobbing grew louder, she repeated, "Justin, you're going to be okay." Finally, he stopped crying and nestled in her arms.

Justin had made a mistake. Alexa had warned him several times earlier not to jump off a railing that was too high, but he did it anyway, which left him holding his left ankle and crying. As Alexa comforted him, she mentioned *nothing* about her warnings. There wasn't even a hint of "I told you so." Instead, all she extended was concern and compassion for her little guy. Justin's pain was her focus, not his mistake. Without thinking about it, Alexa was teaching her son that *we deserve compassion, even if we're the cause of our troubles*.

I was mesmerized as I watched this scene. It was nothing I had ever experienced growing up. I felt a bit of envy as I thought about what Alexa was so compassionately giving her son, something those of us raised in shaming environments must work to give to ourselves. We must work to reject the belief that we don't deserve compassion when we make mistakes, and then we must assemble the words and the feelings of what self-compassion can bring to a weary shame-filled self.

Several days later, I met my same neighbor, Alexa, on the sidewalk as she was returning home. In her hand was a beautiful, small, stuffed dragon. "Oh," I said, "is that a gift?"

"Not really," she told me. "Justin lost his favorite dragon today in the park and has been so upset. We looked and looked for it, but we couldn't find it. So I decided to get him a new one. Things get lost, you know."

What our parents didn't give us

Do you believe you deserve compassion if you cause your own suffering? Probably not. More likely if you are the cause of your own suffering—no compassion for you! We learned to be self-judging and self-condemning, and compassion never crosses our minds. In fact, many raised in a shame-generating family were repeatedly taught that self-compassion is self-pity, self-indulgence, and excuse-making. "Stop feeling sorry for yourself," they might say, making it clear that having compassionate feelings for ourselves is wrong.

But self-compassion is the secret balm to heal the pain of being human. As the above quote by Gilbert (Gilbert 2022) points out, if we haven't received compassion from others, it's something we must learn for ourselves and *consciously* give both to ourselves and others. Self-compassion isn't self-indulgent. Instead, *it is the only way to truly heal.* We may think the best healing agent is the relationship between ourselves and a spouse or a therapist. And indeed, it is essential to feel safe, loved, and understood, but something else is needed too.

The most significant relationship is the one we have with our self, or in parts language, our selves. This is the *attachment bond* we must create. The compassion extended by our spouse, friends, and therapist is important and can be very instrumental in helping us accept ourselves, but it is not as potent as self-compassion. Why? Because when we learn to be self-accepting and self-compassionate, we have learned a vital, life-altering skill that has no expiration date. It is like teaching someone to fish instead of just giving them a trout. We can appreciate and welcome others' compassion, but if we cannot do it for ourselves, we are at a grave disadvantage.

Our many wounded and lost parts burdened by the pain of shame and trauma need *our* understanding and compassion. How we feel about ourselves is more important than how others feel about us. This is likely counter to how you were raised. In many families, what our parents think and feel about us overshadows and informs how we think about ourselves. Appreciating and valuing aspects of ourselves that our parents disapprove of is very difficult. And so we learn early on to turn against ourselves in order to please our parents, rather than appreciate ourselves. And even when we do make the choice to like something about ourselves that our parents don't like—a classic is how we wear our hair—we often struggle with self-doubt.

My client, Peter, was raised in a family where car and motorcycle racing was a way of life. When Peter showed no interest and instead wanted to read and draw, his father was incensed. "I want a boy, not a sissy," Peter remembers his father saying. Not only did his father taunt him, but on one occasion when he found Peter hiding away with a book, his father grabbed the book and threw both book and boy against the wall.

Peter held fast to his inner compass even though he was afraid of his father's anger and disapproval. But he also absorbed some of the self-hate his father fostered. The work we did together helped him unravel those feelings and gradually learn to love and value his many talents. Peter grew up to be a well-respected and much-loved professor of mathematics.

Self-compassion for our "parts"

Let's reflect on a definition of what it means to be healed—to be able to live primarily in the here and now with a sense of peace, ease, and safety. How is this accomplished? Trauma expert Janina Fisher noted that in her many years of experience, "when clients began forming loving attachment bonds to their younger selves, I could see healing at a much deeper level. Seeing them bond with the child they had once been and feeling their shame and self-hatred melt away convinced me that the left brain "adult" side of each one was capable of relating to the right brain "child" side experiencing him or her as innocent and little, spontaneously evoking warmth and protectiveness. Best of all, it was evident that this work was not only transformative but also easy for clients once they learned the basic skills needed to form internal attachment relationships to their parts." (Fisher 2017) This is a powerful observation.

But too often, we hate and disown the parts of us that are in pain. We ignore, deny, and judge them. We are also taught to hate and judge the parts of us that make poor decisions as well as big mistakes. Not only do we suffer from the consequences of that mistake, but we also create a self-condemning inner world where there is no safety or understanding, just hiding, shame, and pain.

My client, Sara, shared the story of telling her mother she was pregnant. She was only fourteen at the time. Without even looking up from the stove, her mother responded, "Well, you got yourself in this mess. Now you figure it out." Years later, in therapy, as Sara befriended the parts of her that made the decision to have sex, she learned that those parts had been repeatedly molested and raped by her uncle. She felt so worthless and used and thought sex was all she was good for. What did Sarah need from her mother when she confided she was pregnant? And now, what does she need from herself? Understanding, belief, and compassion.

Shame confuses us about what we deserve. Shame messages remind us that whatever we are suffering, we brought it on ourselves. When we hear messages like "Maybe this will teach you" or "That's what you get for being so stupid," we believe we deserve no compassion. Or how about "You made your bed; now you can lie in it."

These messages turn us against our parts, those aspects of ourselves that need our understanding and unconditional love. Everyone makes mistakes growing up, and people with a lot of pain inside make more mistakes. Good people do ill-thought-out things—sometimes they get drunk and sometimes pregnant. Maybe not all these decisions are driven by wounded inner parts, but many are, and that's why we need the healing of self-compassion.

Taking time to listen to our upset feelings

Kristin Neff, a pioneer in the study of self-compassion, encourages what she calls a "self-compassion break." (Neff 2015) Too often, she notes, when we're suffering, we just plow ahead. We aren't tuned into our feelings and don't stop to comfort ourselves.

She suggests we take a few moments when we're upset or suffering and become aware that we need special attention. From the "parts" approach perspective, remember that our feelings and moods are messages from our parts. You might ask yourself, "What would the part of me feeling anxious and fearful like me to know? I can feel that you are upset. What is upsetting you? I'd like to be able to help you. How can I help you?" Sometimes just recognizing the feelings of a part is calming.

This differs from our usual approach: "Why the hell am I so anxious? What's wrong with me? Why am I such a wreck?" When we ask those questions, our inner parts hear and feel them. Any wonder why they are sometimes hesitant to connect with us or confide in us? They need our friendship, our understanding, and a safe place to express what they are feeling. We can give them that, and when we do this consistently, we will be rewarded with calmer and happier feelings.

Won't I ever heal?

Let's be clear, the path to healing is not straightforward or easy. This is why we must never give up. When we find old wounds resurfacing, and they will, it is not a setback. Instead, it is a sign that there is more healing to be done. All of us heal in layers, and our wounding often has many layers. Certain experiences and feelings will activate places in our wounding that need our attention. This is often met with discouragement or anger: "What is wrong with me? I thought I was done with this" will likely be our first thoughts. And while no one wants to revisit old sorrowful feelings, do not let these experiences discourage you. In fact, it can be a good sign that your inner healing is progressing. Attend to your distress, compassionately inquire about the part who feels these feelings, and then engage in the process we discussed in Chapter 10 to unburden the little you that needs your healing attention.

Adding self-kindness

Self-kindness is related to self-compassion. They are both heart-motivated actions we engage in for ourselves. Self-kindness is another antidote to the scathing criticism of

shame. But because this may be new for you and contradict what you have thought you deserved, you must *decide*
that you won't feel ashamed for speaking and acting kindly
toward yourself. Don't scold yourself with statements like,
"Aren't you ever happy?" or "Pick yourself up and stop feeling sorry for yourself!" Too often, when you tune in to how
you usually respond to your needs for comfort and kindness,
you'll see that it's often unkind. Now you can learn other
ways to respond.

One way to show self-kindness is through the use of your
own voice. Notice how you feel when you talk to yourself
aloud from a tender place in your heart. And if you use *your
name*, it's even more powerful. Try it now by using your name
and saying something comforting to yourself. For example,
if you don't know what to say, try this: "[Your name], I'm so
proud of you for all you're doing to heal yourself. Good for
you. You're so important to me." What did you notice? Was
it a pleasant experience? Try it again because it may take a
few times before you can open your heart enough to feel it.

You can also make a voice memo on your smartphone or
any recording device. How about recording something for
yourself now? Years ago, when we had answering machines,
I would sometimes call myself and leave a message on my
work machine. I'd try to do this when I knew I had a challenging day ahead. It was a message for my therapist self. I'd
tell her I knew how exhausting her work could be, that she
was doing a good job, and that her work was important. I'd
always end the phone message with, "I love you, Kristine."
When I arrived at my office the following morning, I had
often forgotten about the message. As I listened to my messages before seeing clients, I was surprised to hear my voice.

I'd listen intently, and often I would tear up when I heard the words, "I love you, Kristine."

We know from research that words of kindness trigger our bodies to produce oxytocin and endorphins—the feel-good, feel-calm substances. Oxytocin specifically evokes feelings of safety and warmth toward ourselves and others. When we show kindness and compassion to ourselves, we are giving ourselves what all humans need and want. We are aligning with our heart energy—which is naturally loving, and when we do that, we feel centered and calm.

We may start as strangers to soothing, self-compassion, and self-kindness. It may initially feel silly, awkward, uncomfortable, or even foolishly hopeless. But *these skills are our birthright*, and we need them. We can and must learn to give ourselves something essential to our happiness and well-being, something that we did not get enough of in childhood.

As the calming systems in your brain-body are saturated with endorphins, thinking kind thoughts about yourself becomes easier to access. You are building neuropathways that become like superhighways if you use them frequently enough. But you must intentionally offer these balms to yourself because it won't happen on its own. Can you see that now is your second chance to get these essential skills of self-acceptance and appreciation that you did not get the first go-round? Can you see how essential they are? These are not luxuries, but necessities to help you heal and to smooth life's inevitable ups and downs.

Chapter Takeaways

1. We deserve self-compassion, even when we are responsible for our own suffering or mistakes.
2. Self-compassion is a skill that has no expiration date making it more reliable than external compassion from others. We also need the compassion of others.
3. Self-kindness is a way to counteract shame and self-criticism. Speaking kindly to oneself, especially using one's own voice and name, triggers the production of oxytocin and endorphins and promotes feelings of safety and warmth.

Reflection Question

What situation have you experienced, either recently or in your past, where you could have benefited from giving yourself compassion or kindness? What would you say to yourself if you were to give that gift to yourself?

Practice

1. Remember back to a recent situation where you made a mistake or did something unwise. It could be something minor or more significant.
2. What feelings do you have when you think of this situation? Notice any self-criticism or self-judgment that may come up.
3. Now, imagine that you are speaking to yourself. Use your own name and say something comforting and

supportive. For example, "[Your Name], I know you're going through a tough time, and that's okay. We all make mistakes, and it's a part of being human. I'm here for you, and I care about you."

4. Take a moment to feel the emotions that arise as you offer this kindness to yourself. Pay attention to any shifts in how you feel.

5. Open your eyes and reflect on how it felt to show self-compassion and self-kindness to yourself. Did it feel awkward or uncomfortable at first? Did you notice any changes in your emotional state?

6. Commit to practicing self-compassion and self-kindness regularly, especially when you face challenging situations or make mistakes. Remember that these are essential skills for your well-being and healing.

14

The Wounding of False Mirroring and Projection

Many parents emotionally abuse, neglect, or smother their children by neglecting to practice proper mirroring or by projecting their own unacceptable, rejected qualities onto them.

—Beverly Engel

W e come into life full of light and joy. Yet we don't know who we are. It is through our relationship with our parents that we learn who we are by how they treat us and by what they tell us about ourselves. On our own, we don't know if we are smart, kind, or lovable. Our parents, teachers, siblings, neighbors, and childhood friends tell us. But what if what they tell us is not accurate? We are little sponges to the messages the significant people in our lives send us, and we have no idea if what they tell us is true or colored by their own unhealed wounding.

We spend seventeen to eighteen years with our parents or early caretakers. That's a lot of years during the most vulnerable time in our life. We have limited perspective from which to view our parents' messages and behaviors toward us. We learn to see ourselves based on what they say and how they treat us. Our teachers, coaches, religious leaders, culture, and media influence us too, but the most profound influence happens before we ever get to school.

In psychology, we call this process of learning who we are "mirroring," as in someone holding up a mirror for us to see ourselves. In best cases, it's a valid and kind reflection of our positive traits, areas of talent, and behaviors that need improvement. But if we grow up in a shame-based family, where our parents have a mixed-up sense of who *they* are, mirroring is more like an amusement park mirror—distorted and often unkind. We're unaware of these distortions because we trust adults and believe that what they reflect is genuinely who we are. We have no perspective or ability to think for ourselves until we're older, and by then, the distorted mirroring is deeply planted in our emotional brains.

Later, as we develop the capacity to be self-reflective (around age eight), we may realize this mirroring from authority figures is inaccurate. Still, we're unsure; they may be right. Even if the things they say about us don't feel right, we cannot refute them. We are not strong or independent enough to risk being rejected or hurt. We still need their support. The inaccurate mirroring sticks with us long after the hurt has happened, buried deep within our unconscious and absorbed by our inner "parts." Later, when we want to change those painful messages, we will need more than people telling us the opposite.

Mirror, mirror on the wall

Why was our caretakers' mirroring so painfully off? Because few adults have their emotional world sorted out by the age of eighteen or thirty, or even forty, when they become parents. Young adulthood has many demands and there is little time, and maybe no opportunity or incentive to heal their childhood wounds. These young adults are focused on leaving their family of origin, getting educated, acquiring a skill, maybe beginning a career, and learning how to manage drugs, sex, money, and choosing a suitable mate—whew! And what if these young adults are also parents? With the demands of raising an infant, there is so little time or energy to self-reflect or work on past issues.

Furthermore, you may have grown up with parents who poo-pooed the insights or help of psychology. "I don't need some stranger with a bunch of initials after their name telling me how to fix myself," one client who had been dragged in by his wife told me. In fact, some families believe that introspection is unproductive and even self-centered. "Naval gazing."

So, what do humans do with their negative feelings of unhealed pain? Feelings like self-hate, caustic self-judgment, and unworthiness? They project it onto others. Remember, projection involves unconsciously taking unwanted emotions or traits we don't like about ourselves and attributing them to someone else. It's the mental process by which people attribute what is in *their* minds to *others*. These projections are often the content of the inaccurate mirroring we received.

My client, Cindy, was a young teen when she came home with large hickeys on her neck. Her mother called her a whore. Those words had remained seared in Cindy's beliefs about herself. But when Cindy later learned about projection, she said, "My mother always felt terrible that she had four children by three different men. She tried to keep it a secret because I think she thought that made her a whore."

"And do you think you were a whore?" I asked.

"No, I was a teenager learning about boys, wanting someone to care about me and all that goes with that. But I think my mother thought she was a whore, and she felt very ashamed. So, I guess she projected that onto me. Is that how it works?"

Yes, that's how it works.

Here's a small example from my own life. A friend worried I'd be angry with her because she didn't respond to a holiday message I'd sent to her. Months later, in April, when I invited her to my house for dinner, she told me she had been concerned that I wouldn't want to get together anymore. Instead, I told her I was excited to see her. "I guess *I* was the one feeling so critical of myself for not being a better friend. Pure projection," she said, and we both laughed.

How can parents who carry unresolved wounding and are burdened with shame avoid projecting shame, badness, and brokenness onto their kids? Most often, they can't. Ask yourself what projected, distorted messages you received as a child. Selfish? Fat? Worthless? Damaged? Unlovable? A burden and a bother? Imperfect? Now look at that list and ask yourself if you think these were traits your parent(s) felt about themselves.

My client, Leslie, told me her father often talked about other people being a "zero." Since she has few memories of her father and does not remember any praise or comfort, she was sure he felt that way about her. The fact was that he was a man who gambled, was emotionally disconnected from his wife and children, and had no friends.

Healing false mirroring

Identifying the inaccurate mirroring you received is important, but it's a first step. The second step is to actively reject those false statements, and the third is to replace it with another thought. Here's how that can work:

1. Identify the false statement, such as "you're a whore"; or, in the case of rejection, where there may not have been any words, the parent's or caretaker's rejecting behavior.
2. Ask yourself if your mother or caretaker may have believed this about themselves. Projection of "whore"; or, in the case of rejection, "not worth taking take of."
3. Say out loud with the same confidence you'd use to reject a statement that you're a serial murderer, "I reject this. This isn't mine. It does not belong to me. It is not true."
4. Using your mother's, caretaker's, or offender's first name, say aloud "Loretta, this is your issue." (Sometimes, you may not be able to identify the projection's origins. That's okay; you can just imagine throwing the accusation out into the air like you'd throw a ball of lies as far away from you as you could.)
5. Say again, with all the determination you can muster, "I reject this. It isn't mine. I reject it."

6. This last step is critical. It's important to claim a "truth" about yourself that does feel true. What feels true to you may change over time. About the whore accusation, maybe you begin with the statement, "I let boys take advantage of me. I wish I hadn't." Maybe you can say with confidence, "What's true is that I made some decisions I now look back on with regret, but I can also see how lost I was." "I was lost, not a whore." Maybe, in time, "The decisions I made about sex are not the sum of me. I was young and unloved, and I was seeking acceptance the only way I knew how. I'm a good person."

The point is to gradually claim your own understanding and perspective about who you are intrinsically. This is your own truth about yourself. Reject the lies others have thrown on you. They don't belong to you.

How did you do? Did you say it with conviction? Was your voice strong and determined? If you sounded unsure or your voice trailed up as it does when we ask a question, repeat the exercise until you feel like *I have this*.

Each time you are aware of a projection, a false mirroring label or a belief you have about yourself (and there will be hundreds of times), repeat this exercise. It's important to say it aloud with fierce determination. If it helps, think of how crippling and damaging this message has been to you. Think of how believing the false mirroring has influenced your decisions. (Since I'm a whore, I have no worth, and boys or men can do what they want to me. Since no one wants me, I should be grateful that anyone wants to be with me. I can't be choosey.) Let yourself become angry if you can. (Anger is a healthier emotion than shame or defeat.) Attributing false, derogatory attributes to you was a cruel thing to do to you, even if it was unintentional. Rejecting them as not accurate about you with conviction is essential.

If you feel unsure about the mirroring and find yourself thinking maybe it was true, have a little chat with yourself. Do not wait for all of you to believe the false projections are untrue. Instead, focus on the parts of you that know the truth—your wise mind and speak from that part. Later, you may need to engage that young part of you that continues to believe falsehoods and engage her in a healing dialogue described in the chapter on befriending parts lost in the past.

Can you see why immature parents or those with a lot of unhealed pain can't accurately mirror who you are? Tragically, when these unhealed parents believe their projections are accurate, they often feel justified in their hurtful, even cruel, treatment of their children.

Throughout our life, we will have many people mirroring how they perceive us. And while it's important to be around those who are kind and supportive, everyone will see you through their own stuff. As Beverly Engel points out in her book devoted entirely to working with mirroring, "Because the mirrors of everyone may contain some distortions, as did your parents' mirroring, these other views of you may not be accurate." (Engel 2006)

Treasuring the good

So how do you get an accurate picture of yourself? As we weed out negative messages we received as children, we need to fill in the void with observations from others that are accurate mirroring. This is most important. How do we do this? By treasuring all positive messages others give us, even if we believe they're too good to be true. This is the beginning of how we can build an accurate sense of who we are. Yes, it is a challenge for the shame-prone because our internalized shame-speak will try to upend our attempts to hear and hold on to positive reflections. As a result, shame becomes its own sorting mechanism: the bad stays and the good is disbelieved and tossed.

But when we know how shame works, we have the upper hand. You'll recall that shame was a protective survival response that kept us safe by making us non-assertive and non-combative. In shame, we are small, collapsed, and submissive. But when we begin to believe we are worthy of respect, protection, and being loved and valued, shame gradually loses its grip. But we may feel uneasy and even afraid of seeing ourselves in this light. Why? From a parts perspective, the parts that have kept us small and passive by telling us, "Don't get too full of yourself! Who do you think you are?" will become fearful that we will be hurt. They still live in the past and continue to believe that we live in an unsafe world where everyone will betray and hurt us. These parts will warn us through feelings and thoughts insisting we need to stay deflated and compliant.

But we have other choices. We can gradually collect the positive mirroring others offer us. We can talk to our parts, reassuring them that we are safe now as adults and deserve to feel good about ourselves. When we become aware of our tendency to shrug off positive things people say about us, we can choose instead to collect and treasure those messages. But we must make a conscious effort. It won't happen on its own.

I've watched many shame-prone clients visibly shrug their shoulders as I offered them an accurate mirroring of something positive about them. I often make the analogy that everyone has a basket inside them to hold the positive things people say, and through no error on their part, their basket appears to have a hole in the bottom. "Plug up the hole," I tell them. "Every positive thing people say to you is a beautiful gift. Hold on to it. Treasure it. Be open to the possibility that *these beautiful statements mirror who you truly are.*"

When I began my concerted effort to plug up the many holes in my own bucket and accept others' positive mirroring, I started noticing how others reacted when someone complimented them. Over and over, I heard them say a quick and sincere "thank you." Even though I wasn't yet convinced that the compliments or mirroring I received were genuine, I decided to make this my response, too. I started just saying, "thank you."

Try this. Anytime someone says anything positive, thank them. And remember, you deserve to hold a positive image of yourself even if your behavior isn't always terrific. This is the critical distinction between self and behavior. Shame tells us that because our behavior is sometimes unkind, unfair, dumb, ill-thought-out, or even mean, those behaviors equate to being a defective person. That's simply not true. You are more than your behavior, even when you make big mistakes.

Despite what your parents or caretakers have said about you, regardless of how they or anyone else treated you, remember, again, that nothing comes from heaven broken. You were born worthy of love and respect, and nothing has changed that.

—·—

Chapter Takeaways

1. Mirroring begins even before we can understand language. Our emotional brains and nervous systems register the feelings and attitudes of significant adults. As we grow older, and understand language, their words add another layer to our self-image.
2. In families where parents have unhealed shame and unresolved issues, mirroring can gives us a skewed self-image because we trust these adults and believe their reflections to be true. Recognizing and addressing distorted mirroring is essential for us to be able to reject these messages.
3. Parents often project their unresolved emotions and disliked traits onto us. Understanding projection can help us refuse to accept the projection and recognize when others might be projecting their stuff onto us.
4. To counteract negative messages from childhood, we must actively seek and treasure positive mirroring from others. This means accepting compliments and positive feedback, even if our internalized shame resists. Over time, this can help us build a more accurate and positive self-image. While this sounds simple, it is critical.

Reflection Question

What are two traits that your best friends see in you that you have trouble seeing in yourself? How can you begin to accept that their mirroring could be accurate reflections?

Practice

1. Set aside this week to focus on gracefully accepting compliments and positive feedback.
2. Whenever someone says something positive about you, no matter whether you believe it or not, no matter how small or insignificant it may seem to you, respond with a sincere "thank you." Don't deflect or downplay the compliment.
3. How does it feel to acknowledge and accept positive reflections from others? This practice can help you become more comfortable with receiving positive mirroring and as it adds up and contradicts some of the negative messages you got, it will gradually build a more positive self-image. Now isn't that something you'd like to have?

15

Why It's Difficult to Trust

Being able to feel safe with other people is probably the single most important aspect of mental health.

—Bessel van der Kolk

One of toxic shame's greatest weapons is its ability to convince us that our brokenness is so obvious that unless we keep people at a distance, they'll discover how damaged we are. And if they do get close to us, we're confident they won't want to be our friend, our workplace team member, and certainly not our romantic partner. To protect ourselves from being discovered as the not-good-enough self we believe ourselves to be, we hide our vulnerabilities and present an acceptable stand-in persona, or false self. But because we know this public self is an edited version of who we believe we are, we're haunted by feelings of being a fake and an imposter.

Often, our lives of being hurt, betrayed, unwanted, and not valued have also convinced us that others are not to be trusted. As a way to protect us from being further hurt, we may have adopted the idea that we don't really need anyone.

This mistrust and fear of others puts us in a terrible bind because connection with other people is hardwired into our DNA. When we look at this from an evolutionary background, our species survived by forming groups that could contribute to each member's welfare. We learned to work together for the greater good, procreate together, and provide protection for each other. Inclusion in the group meant we were valued and belonging to a group meant survival. The alternative was bleak. If our group rejected us, we would not survive. We needed and continue to need other people.

As humans, we call the part of our brain that seeks and needs affiliation the mammalian brain structure. The mammalian brain compels us to form community and to reach out to others for support and value. Unfortunately, when we are traumatized, or in an overwhelming state of fear, our mammalian brain shuts off, leaving us to function with a more primitive brain structure, our reptilian brain. This early brain structure makes us feel safe when alone and hostile when we feel someone trying to get close to us. This is the brain of solitary reptiles, like those blue-belly lizards you see on hikes or in your backyard in summer. To get a visual of this, Van der Kolk suggested we visit any pet store and observe how the animals act. In the mammal section of rabbits, kittens, rats, or puppies, we will notice that they pile together in a little heap when they feel either scared or safe. Snakes or lizards, on the contrary, remain alone and solitary whether in a state of fear or safety. (Van der Kolk 2014) Humans are capable of both, and the choice is often made unconsciously. Our reptilian brain overtakes us when we are in a survival mode or believe we are threatened or unsafe.

Slipping into our reptilian brain is often unfortunate. We are, after all, innately social beings, and our mammalian brains are built to help us function as members of a tribe. However, with repeated trauma, the reptilian brain takes charge. Often our reptilian nervous system doesn't accurately assess whether we're safe or in danger. As a result, we may feel in danger or scared of people when there is nothing to fear. As Van der Kolk wrote, "While the smoke detector in our brains is pretty good at picking up danger clues, trauma increases the risk of misinterpreting whether a particular situation is dangerous or safe. And accurately assessing whether someone's intentions are harmless or dangerous is essential for our complex relationships at work, home, or community." (Van der Kolk 2014) When our ability to assess others for safety (are they friend or foe) is compromised, both children and adults can find themselves caught in the painful push-pull of needing people on the one hand and fearing them on the other hand.

The lies that confused us

Shame-inducing families too often teach their children to put up with unpredictable, unloving, and untrustworthy people. Awful behavior from family members and friends is accepted or tolerated. As one of my female clients told me, "We all knew Grandpa liked to pinch our nipples. Even my mother knew, and when I tried to tell her about it, she said he'd always been like that. So, we tried to stay away from him. But when he caught us off guard, we just laughed it off. As my mother said, 'That's just Grandpa.'"

When another client's mother got upset, which was frequently, she often called her and her sister whores and sluts. Their dad would later reassure them, "She didn't really mean it. She loves you two." When cruelty and emotional abuse are minimized and when you are told that your offenders love you, what is your picture of love?

These misleading and deceitful messages also contribute to our confusion about setting limits on unacceptable behavior from our friends and family. Add to this our sense of unworthiness, and it's easy to see that we're set up for a string of chaotic and unhappy relationships.

The worst lies deny our own experiences or contradict our intuition. We're born with a "gut sense" or intuition designed to guide us, especially about who and what is dangerous. These messages from our intuition are subtle, often manifesting as feelings or a hunch—things our brain can't explain. Nonetheless, these messages are powerful pieces of information ... a sixth sense that we need as much as we need our eyes and ears. Our five senses and intuition are designed to help us and keep us safe.

When parents insist that their perceptions and what they say is true, even when it contradicts our intuition, we get confused. It certainly seems safest for us to believe our parents. Imagine trying to correct them or refusing to go along with their falsehoods. What do we do as children? We override our intuition, and we go along with our parents and other authority figures ... coaches, religious leaders, teachers.

After a time, we become so far removed from our intuition and oftentimes even suspect that our intuition is wrong: we lose our way. What do we do then? We rely on others to tell us what is right or wrong, good or bad, or safe or dangerous. We rely on them to tell us who we are. We give up on our own internal guidance system as we try to please them and make peace. This is impossible, of course, because everyone has different perspectives and firm beliefs about who we are and what we should do and be. We become anxious and more lost.

How can you regain access to your intuition? This question is important and one I encourage you to explore beyond this brief mention. One step is to intentionally notice and listen to your intuition's messages. These messages often come in the form of feelings. We often do this in hindsight: "Something told me that wasn't a good idea. I had this terrible feeling, but I went ahead anyway." The more you are aware of your intuitive message, even in hindsight, the more accessible the messages will be. It's like learning to tune into a particular radio station. But even when you hear your intuition, it can be tough to follow the advice.

For example, a young client who grew up in a family full of lies had a terrible time following her intuition's guidance. It wasn't that she didn't hear it; it was just that following it often meant going against her family. She had frequently been punished and accused by her mother of being a troublemaker whenever she questioned the unfair treatment or contradictory modeling in her family. To survive in her family, she had protective inner parts that warned her that listening to her intuition was dangerous. This fear of following her inner guidance persisted when she left her family. She had to learn, often the hard way, that her intuition was actually her friend.

When, as children, we're scolded and punished for blurting out our unfiltered intuition and perceptions, such as

"Grandpa is nasty," we learn to override and eventually ignore our perceptions. It feels too risky. This is a terrible and dangerous loss. It's like being blinded in one eye. If this happened to you, consider whether you'd like to get reacquainted with your intuition as a potential friend.

We can all get better tuned into our intuition, or inner guidance, by noticing how things turn out when we ignore the messages our GPS sends us. This is motivation through pain, the ill effects of ignoring the wisdom of intuition. It's also possible to dial into our intuition by choice and avoid the pain. We can ask for guidance. We can value our feelings and know that when we feel uneasy, when someone or something makes our hair stand on end, or we feel queasy and sick, those can be warnings from our precious personal GPS.

Blind loyalty: the glue of unhealthy families

My client, Rose, grew up in a family where the adults gambled, partied, fought, and freely asked each other for money. It was always posited as a loan. If a family member refused, they were bad-mouthed and accused of being selfish. When Rose became an adolescent and left home, her older brother started asking her for loans from the money she made boarding horses. Rose always said "yes," even when it cut into her rent money. She always got burned, however, because she really didn't have the money to lend, and he never repaid her. But she thought this was what family does for each other. Rose knew she was being taken advantage of and knew she needed to say no, but she didn't. She thought this was the price of having a family. When she turned fifty, Rose received from her brother a small box filled with a stack of fifty crisp one-dollar bills. She carefully counted them and, for a few days, was tempted to believe her brother had lovingly remembered her birthday. A week later, he called and asked her for a $500 loan. She told him no. He got angry, called her names, and told her he was "through." Rose felt hurt, but she also felt empowered.

In some families, there's an unwritten rule about family lies—never question them. We're taught to follow the three-monkey approach—see no evil, hear no evil, speak no evil. Whether we have explicit memories or not, we were likely schooled not to see through the lies of our family. It's a loyalty issue. And going against the family loyalty rules can result in having no family.

Shame-prone people get caught in loyalty binds, love-hate bonds, minimization, and outright denial, which swirl in the family craziness. Because this is associated with survival, family loyalty is practically in your DNA. As clients caught in loyalty binds would tell me as they began to talk about their family, "I didn't come here to throw my mother under the bus." A big part of adulthood is emancipating emotionally from your parents. Part of emancipating is seeing and acknowledging the truth about your experiences and your parents. It doesn't need to be unloving, but it does need to be truthful.

Your only loyalty needs to be to yourself and your own healing, not minimizing others' harmful behavior and perpetuating the lies you were raised with. Your family may label you as selfish, uppity, ungrateful, and a few obscenities. The fear of losing members of your family is real. One way around this bind is to pick friends to be your family and keep your relatives from controlling you. This may be the price of your emotional freedom.

The lobster effect

I once read that if you have at least two lobsters in a bucket, you do not have to worry that they will climb out and escape. Why? Because the minute one tries to climb up the bucket side, the other will grab it and pull it back into the bucket. None of them will get free.

Shame-generating families can be like this, too. When you choose to leave the family "bucket" and cultivate healthy friends, promising careers, and loving partners, your family members may accuse you of being too special or disloyal. Have you ever been told, "Who do you think you are?" That is the same as "Get back in this bucket with the rest of us. This is what family does." The verbal message may be "we look out for each other," but the actual behaviors can be the opposite.

Our families or friends may wrongly believe they are looking out for us, but in truth, they may be imposing their values and their severely pruned dreams onto us. They believe they are worrying for our safety, our souls, or the wisdom of our desires and decisions. Sometimes our family believes we owe them, which means staying close and helping them make their lives okay, even to our detriment.

My client, Rhonda, told me that as a teen she was an excellent student who studied hard for her upcoming SAT exams, knowing her score could open scholarship opportunities to good colleges. She was proud that she would be the first in her family to go to college. But the night before her big test, her father came home late, drunk. Bursting into her bedroom where she was sleeping, he yanked her out of bed, got right in her face, and yelled, "You think you're too good for us? We sacrificed for you, and this is the thanks we get! Go take that goddam exam, but you're not going anywhere."

When we leave behind dysfunctional patterns and piece together our own values, we may feel a pang of guilt we don't understand. But as I've told my clients many times, guilt isn't always about doing something we shouldn't do. Sometimes, we feel guilty when we violate a loyalty bind. We must not let that kind of guilt stop us. Instead, we can identify our loyalty binds and by making them conscious, we can eventually be free of them. When the blinders are off or less opaque, we can begin to see people in our lives for who they are and discern whether they have our best interests at heart. Even then, as you'll see in the next chapter, we need to learn a few more things.

———

Chapter Takeaways

1. Toxic shame can lead us to hide our vulnerabilities and present a false self to others. We may think this false self makes us more acceptable, but it leaves us feeling like impostors and fakers.

2. Our brains have evolved to seek affiliation and connection (mammalian brain) but can also become defensive and solitary (reptilian brain) in response to trauma or fear, whether it is true danger or not.

3. Our intuition, often expressed as gut feelings or hunches, can guide us in identifying danger or discomfort in relationships. Learning to recognize and trust our intuition is vital. No one knows more about what is good for us than intuition-informed guidance.

4. Loyalty to unhealthy family patterns and the fear of breaking away from them can lead to blind loyalty and self-sacrifice. Emancipating emotionally from such patterns and seeking your own truth as an adult are the requirements of being mature.

Reflection Question

Has loyalty always been a good thing in your family?

Practice

Take out your notebook.

1. Identify one loyalty bind you have broken free of. These are some possible examples:

    *   Leaving a family religion despite your family protests.
    *   Choosing a career other than the one your parents want you to pursue.
    *   Staying true to your sexual orientation when your parents believe it is wrong or a sin.
    *   Separating from family members who do not support your growth and emotional well-being.

- Dating or marrying someone of your choosing.
- Bettering yourself through education or employment even if family members consider it disloyal and uppity.

2. How did you do this? What traits and strengths did you find within yourself? Who supported your efforts?
3. Were there consequences?
4. Was it worth it?

16

The Challenges of Choosing Healthy Relationships

From the cradle to the grave, humans desire a certain someone who will look out for them, notice and value them, soothe their wounds, reassure them in life's difficult places, and hold them in the dark.

—Susan M. Johnson

One day a divorced client tearfully discussed how lonely she had felt for years. Although she longed for someone to share her life with, she feared it wasn't possible. I empathized with her feelings and then suggested that her loneliness could be a motivation to begin dating again. "Look," she said, "every relationship I've ever had has ended in rejection. I'm no dummy—the only constant is me. I'm the problem. Something is wrong with me, and I'm not going through it again."

I have often heard this self-assessment, "something is wrong with me." Some believed they were too broken. Many unconsciously believed their profound sense of unworthiness meant they had to settle for anyone who showed them attention. Others said their "picker was broken" or that they were cursed. But as I got to know these clients, I noticed that they didn't suffer from "broken pickers" or being cursed. They were confused and misguided in choosing friends and romantic partners because they were drawn to the wrong person.

We may think our primary motivation in dating or entering a committed relationship is to choose happiness and love, but we are unknowingly marching to two drummers who may not lead us in the direction we desire. First, we will seek what is familiar, even if it's not good for us. Second, we will seek out potential partners based on false ideas of who we believe we are. Believing "I'm not worthy," for example, sets us up to not be valued in the relationship. But when we are aware of our patterns, we can begin to do the work to change them.

Being raised in shame-generating families often equates to experiencing a series of troubled relationships. We can't help it. For example, if you believe you're lucky to find someone who wants to be with you, you will cling to that relationship even if it's unhealthy. You will blame yourself for the troubles in the relationship and likely stay in the relationship until he or she breaks up with you. Now you have one more proof that everyone rejects you. Of course, we can learn from these "failures," but we often get lost in the pain. Over time, we become discouraged, even hopeless. We believe the failed relationships are further proof of our defects and unworthiness. This is especially true in romantic relationships.

Choosing the familiar

We all unconsciously choose what's familiar. Those but-terflies you feel—the sense that you know this person and they're perfect for you—are often the whisperings and prompts from parts within your psyche. Younger versions of yourself are drawn to people with habits and characteristics similar to your parents. This would be fine if your childhood parental relationships were a source of love and happiness, but when the emotional patterns were unhealthy, even if they're familiar, you must learn to make other choices.

For example, if you grew up with a needy and depressed mother who relied on you to cheer her up and keep the fam-ily running, you may be drawn to someone who is struggling emotionally. It's familiar, and you know how to put your needs aside and focus on others. Or if one of your parents was an alcoholic, you may be drawn to someone who has a drinking problem. One of my clients told me she was drawn to a boyfriend because she loved the way he smelled. As she got to know him better, she realized his scent was the smell of Jack Daniels, the same bourbon her father drank. Even someone who has a scary temper can feel familiar. Many other unhealthy emotional patterns are also familiar—con-trolling, smothering, critical, demeaning, and emotionally unavailable.

Probably the most common dynamic is choosing some-one who, for some reason, does not and cannot love you. Shame-prone adults often have a distorted or incomplete sense of what love is and how love feels. We aren't con-scious of this as we choose our romantic partners, but if you reflect, you may realize that your parents, despite their best intentions, did not know how to love their children. Your parents' own childhood wounds created barriers and limited their capacity for the openhearted, unconditional love children need. When as an adult you still feel an emptiness and longing for love, you may unconsciously choose someone who, sadly, like your parents, is not capable of it.

Why would we pick someone with unhealthy emotional patterns, especially if these are the very traits that made us feel awful about ourselves growing up? Freud had a theory about this. He called it "repetition compulsion." His theory was that we choose *emotionally familiar* people because familiarity suggests safety. But an equally compelling reason, Freud suggested, is that we're seeking a do-over. We want to get the love and acceptance that we couldn't get from our parents, and we believe, unconsciously, that we can now change what we couldn't change as a child. We can finally find a way to make the other person approve of us. Without being aware of what we're doing, we act as though our romantic partner is a stand-in for the parent whose love and approval we never got.

Not knowing what we're attempting and how impossible this is, we hope that the aloof or self-focused person we date or choose as a partner will, because of our love, eventually come around and see our worth. Or, for example, we want the familiar, angry date or partner to see how much we love them, and stop being so mad. And even though we feel broken and unlovable, we hope the familiar, emotionally distant, and unavailable sweetheart will find us worthy of their attention and love.

Unfortunately, despite our best efforts, which may last for decades, the magic we hoped we could perform doesn't happen. Why? Because we aren't the source of our romantic partner's problems, just as we weren't the source of our parents' lack of love and protection. Many parents believe it is up to the child to alter their behavior to positively affect their experience. Children are often blamed for their parents' unhappiness and told explicitly that if they would do as they were told—be better kids, get better grades, be more helpful, pick up after themselves, or stop fighting with their siblings—then the parents wouldn't be so angry all the time and they'd be more loving. This puts the responsibility for how the parent feels on the child. What child can see that this is not true? Maybe even now as you read this you are questioning this premise. We know this is not true because we see parents who are irritated with their misbehaving children, who are exhausted from the fighting and quarreling but who are still loving and able to separate bad behavior from bad kids. Their love is unconditional.

We weren't the source of our parents' difficulty with being loving, and we are also not the source of our romantic partner's guarded or closed hearts. We are also not the source of the healing these familiar people need. Their healing must come from within them, because that is where they carry their wounding. We don't have a chance. The only antidote to our repeated disappointments and hurt is to extend compassion to ourselves and to learn to recognize our patterns so we can change them. We didn't understand that this mission we undertook to win the love we never had was impossible, and now we deserve our own loving shoulder to cry on.

We also need to educate ourselves about the many people who can be described as empathy deficient. "Some people are not wired neurologically or emotionally to have empathy. Behavioral scientists define this condition as "empathy deficient disorder" where someone focuses on their own needs and neglects or doesn't care about the feelings of others. Those with empathy deficient disorder lack a moral compass." (Orloff 2024) Many of my clients, unaware that this disorder exists, got caught up in romantic relationships with someone who could not love them. As Orloff explains, the ability to care about others occurs on a spectrum. On one end is the highly sensitive person who may find she tunes into others with no effort at all. She may believe that most people can be like her if they really try. One the other end of the spectrum are the pathological narcissists, sociopaths, and psychopaths. According to a study reported in a psychiatry journal, the occurrence of narcissistic personality disorder is 7 per 100, with more men than women in this category. (Stinson 2008) If you are involved with someone who is selfish, says all their ex-partners were crazy and accuses you of being over reactive, irrational and lacks empathy for your pain and distresses, you may be dealing with a pathological narcissist. How do you recognize a sociopath? According to Martha Stout, they are rule breakers, (the rules and laws don't pertain to them), and who con and exploit others without regard or remorse. They lie, borrow money, cheat and refuse to take responsibility. Prevalence is said to be 3 in 100 men and 1 in 100 females. (Stout 2005) Psychopaths are an extreme version of sociopaths occurring at the rate of 1.2 per 100 in men and .03–.07 per 100 in women. If these behaviors remind you of someone, see the Resource section of this book and educate yourself. Seek out other sources as well because it's important to be aware. Perhaps you will find that your family tree has a few of these folks. And remember you will be miserable if you think you can change them.

Should we be cautious of the familiar? We don't need to be black or white, but again we need to be aware. When we feel attracted to someone, even though we may believe romantic love shouldn't involve careful analysis, we need to remember that an enduring and healthy love consists of both head and heart. What we may believe is our intuition can be clouded by many factors. "Repetition compulsion" is our young, inner parts being actively engaged in our relationships or dating choices and sending messages and sensations. The adult part of us must be aware of the influence of our younger selves, because this younger part may be yearning for something familiar that isn't in our best interest. One way you can determine if you are under the influence of a younger part is by asking yourself how old you feel when you are thinking about a potential romantic person. Do you sometimes feel younger than your age? Do you find yourself feeling different ages at various times? This is not uncommon, but it is a potential problem if your early life was replete with emotionally unhealthy patterns.

Identifying our patterns

Becoming aware is the first step to changing our relationship patterns. You can do this by identifying your reoccurring patterns. Start by making a list of the painful and disappointing experiences you have had repeatedly. Maybe you have a pattern of giving more in a relationship than you get back. You may hear yourself thinking, *If I do this for him, he'll like me more and be more invested in the relationship.* Or you may recognize a pattern of minimizing or ignoring that he fails to follow through on commitments he makes to you or just doesn't seem to remember the important things you share with him like the dynamics you have with your boss, or the health concerns you're worried about, maybe even forgets your birthday. Putting up with things you don't like and hoping you can change the other person is a common pattern. Some of us are like the SPCA: "Bring me your unwanted and abandoned, and I will love them back to health." Love is very powerful, but I don't think we can love someone back to a healthy mental state. Our love may provide a platform, but the healing and the work must come from them.

To get a clear sense of one of your patterns, close your eyes and focus on one of your not-so-healthy reoccurring patterns. Patterns are behaviors that express a belief you hold. Take, for example, these beliefs: *I have to please others so they will love me. Everyone ultimately rejects me. Caretaking is my ticket to getting someone to care about me. I'll take what I can get.* When you become aware of a belief you hold, and there may be several, write them down. These beliefs are the sense you made of your experiences with your parents or primary caretaker as you tried to understand why they didn't love you or cherish you in a way that felt secure and reliable. These beliefs are old, deep, and often unconscious.

These false beliefs about yourself then become the unconscious template for the friends and partners you choose. For example, the pattern of always trying to win the love of the person you're dating comes from a belief that just being yourself is not enough. This mindset may also caution you not to be disagreeable and to concede in order to please them, that if you disagree or upset your partner, they will become angry and leave you. Over-focusing on how another person feels about you may also distract you from attending to how you feel about them. Identifying your beliefs puts them into your awareness and from there you can work on them.

The next step is one that is often overlooked. Consider the possibility that by showing up in relationships in ways that reflect what you believe about yourself, you are sending a message that this is how you expect to be treated. For example, if you believe you're not worthy of attention and affection, you probably send that message and attract men or women who are predisposed to be inattentive, either because of being over-committed, emotionally preoccupied because of their own struggles, or unavailable because their family of origin's dysfunction and drama is never-ending. When you are unhappy about being treated this way, it's also likely that you don't speak up about your needs. And because you don't speak up, the other person will continue to treat you like you don't have those needs. Furthermore, by not speaking up, the other person misses out on a chance to change how they treat you. When you speak up, it's certainly possible that nothing will change, and that's disappointing. But now you know you have given them the heads-up.

My client, Jammie, was working to identify her beliefs about herself and how they showed up in her relationships. She realized that she believed she was lucky if anyone cared about her. She also realized that she was continuing to act on a piece of advice her mother had instilled: "Give a man whatever he wants sexually if you want to keep him." As a result, she often felt sexually used in her adult relationships.

But she didn't speak up, fearful she'd lose the relationship. Instead, she believed all men were only out for themselves sexually.

Another client identified a pattern of "accepting breadcrumbs." She knew she often felt unworthy, but she did not connect the dots between this self-assessment and how she showed up in her relationships. Instead, she had blamed the men for being selfish and thoughtless.

What to do about these insights? You can intentionally change the pattern by showing up differently. When you get the "breadcrumb" feeling, ask yourself how someone who feels worthy of respect and reciprocity would address the situation. Remember, you are changing a pattern in *yourself, not someone else.* Yes, some people are selfish, but sometimes it's because you haven't spoken up about your needs. And if you have spoken up, give some thought to a way to deliver the message so they can hear you and not become defensive. After years of hiding or minimizing your feelings, it is often difficult to find the words, and even then, the years of anger and resentment going all the way back to childhood color our delivery. Being accusatory, angry, demanding, or just putting up with it is not how to convey your needs. Learning how to bring up your needs and preferences so the other person is not thrown into defensiveness is a skill you can learn.

If you are currently in an unhappy relationship and suspect it may be emotionally abusive, I suggest you read Beverly Engel's book *Escaping Emotional Abuse: Healing from the Shame You Don't Deserve.* In this insightful book, Engel asks questions to help you determine if your relationship is emotionally abusive. (Key: you often feel put down, criticized, demeaned, and dismissed.) She also compassionately addresses how difficult it is to leave such a relationship and offers support and guidance. (Engel 2020)

Often, we don't know how to create a healthy relationship or even what one looks like. John Gottman is a psychologist and researcher who is well known for their research on what makes healthy romantic relationships. He has followed hundreds of couples, gay and straight, over many years studying what makes relationships work and what causes them to fall apart. His research suggests that how we go about bringing up our needs so that the conversation or request goes well is critical to healthy communication and something we can all learn. When people become defensive or want to leave the conversation, it is likely that we have used a "harsh start-up," an approach that is guaranteed to go poorly. (John Gottman 2015)

Beginning with a harsh start-up goes something like this: "I asked you to get a birthday card for our friend. I even texted to remind you and here you are with no card. Why can't you remember anything? I guess you expect me to do everything just like I always do." We can see why that approach isn't going to go well. But what is an alternative? A more successful way is, "I see you don't have a card for our friend. I'm upset that so much of our social connections fall to me. Could you please get a card tomorrow?" It is easy to see that the non-accusatory approach is much more likely to go well.

If your partner gets defensive, you may have been accusatory. Words like "you always" and "you never" are fighting words, and, generally, they're inaccurate. But when we are upset, it is difficult to not just launch in with criticism. There is another way worth learning. And just like any new skill, you will need to practice. The formula is: complaint based on facts, your feelings, and your request for a remedy. I recommend Gottman's books, and other works by Gottman, because the principles he discusses are research based, with real couples. I can personally attest to how helpful these concepts have been to me and many of my clients.

You also need some models. Who in your life or who in a movie or TV show uses words or phrases that you'd like to adopt. Remember them. Write down the words or phrases and practice them. I remember going with my stepfather to Sears, where he wanted to return a lawn edging tool. I watched as he approached the clerk and heard him say something like "this thing doesn't work. I want my money back, and if you don't give it to me, I will take my business to Montgomery Wards." Even at fourteen, I knew there had to be better ways, and I wanted to learn them. I paid attention to others who knew how to navigate potentially tricky situations with finesses and grace. Those were the examples I tried to incorporate in my life. I memorized the phrases, but I also learned that approaching someone with respect and an expectation that we would work this out amicably was key.

If you're generally not one to bring up something that you fear is contentious or difficult, begin by practicing in non-risky situations. "This salmon looks undercooked to me. Can I have it cooked a little more, please?" you might say to the waiter. "Can I get someone to carry this case of water to my car? I'd really appreciate it," to the person bagging your groceries. When you get some practice, begin to express your needs with friends. Beware, you may lose some friends. They may not want to be friends with someone who speaks up for themselves. But this is the direction you must go to change the experiences you have in your life. Finally, be brave, because your happiness depends on it, and begin to speak up in your closest relationships. Again, you may lose some folks, but you won't lose yourself.

Identifying what you do want

What should we be looking for if not someone familiar? Answer: someone who is emotionally available and knows how to love and care for others. How will we know? We can get some clues by looking at their other relationships. For example, how do they speak about and care for their mother, sister, or brother? Even if they aren't close, are they respectful and fair when they talk about them? And importantly, do they have solid, long-term healthy friendships that they value and nurture?

My client, Stanley, came to see me to sort out his feelings about a woman he had dated for a number of months. Stanley was ready for a committed relationship and was tired of starting over. He wanted to salvage this one if he could. But as he talked in detail about this relationship, he recognized that he had overlooked a number of red flags. His current girlfriend didn't have friends, and he was aware that she didn't express missing him when he was away on business trips. He had seen all this, but he had minimized how significant these markers were. Instead, he told himself, "Oh, she's too busy at work to have the time or energy for friends. I do wish she would tell me she missed me, but she said she doesn't want to focus on negative things." Looking back,

Stanley realized the excuses he made for her were reflective of his "breadcrumb" beliefs that had crept up again. He was determined to speak up a bit more.

When Stanley did talk about his concerns, he was pleased that his girlfriend seemed to listen. But several days later, she texted and ended the relationship. Stanley was angry, but he also realized he needed more from her, and if she couldn't give it, the relationship needed to end. He just wished he'd been the one to end it.

Every relationship has elements you like and aspects you don't want. To purposefully assemble your template for relationships you want, your job is to recognize the behaviors, feelings, and experiences you like and want to have repeated. This is contrary to how most of us reflect on past "unsuccessful" relationships. Instead, we are predisposed to focus on what we didn't like. While this review is useful, it's *critical* that we follow up those negative assessments with what we do want. Knowing what we do want is powerful. Think about going to a department store. If you know what you want, aren't you more likely to find it than if your focus is on all the things you don't want?

Have you heard the phrase, "What you focus on expands?" Here's an example: When I lived in Sacramento, I was often on the freeways with lots of semi-trucks making their way through town. I thought they were mostly good drivers who just needed a certain amount of space to maneuver their big rigs. However, in contrast, I noticed that some of my clients would complain about how rude and inconsiderate truck drivers were. Their experience was the opposite of my own. How could we have such different experiences?

Was it what we focused on? Were these clients more focused on the negative than I was? One thing is for sure: what we believe is true is what we notice.

When asked to describe the relationship qualities we prefer, many of us have a short or not very specific list. Sometimes we're embarrassed to really put it out there: "I want someone who listens and respects me, who supports my dreams and cares for me deeply, and toward whom I feel the same way." Repeatedly thinking about what you didn't like does not create a template of what you do want. Make your custom list inclusive of all the good you've experienced in past relationships, even ones that didn't work out, and include things you want to repeat in your future relationships. Include what you have seen and admired in the relationships of others. When you're standing in the grocery line and you see a kind exchange between the clerk and a customer, ask for that. If you're listening to a song and you like the sentiment, ask for that. Your job is to have a list of what you want that is long and specific. If you're watching a series on TV and the characters are mistreating each other, ask for the opposite. "I want to be treated with respect, even when we disagree."

One of my clients described leaving her marriage of several years even though she found her husband to be a lot of fun. But he was also messy, irresponsible, and unfocused on his career. She wanted to start a family. She wanted a husband who was responsible. The next man she was attracted to was an engineer for a company in her building. "What attracted you to him?" I asked. "When I saw that his desk was all organized and orderly, I thought, this guy is responsible, he has a good job, and he is neat and orderly." But as she dated him, she learned that he wasn't fun. He took his responsibilities seriously, which she appreciated, but she realized that being able to laugh and have some goofy care-free times were important too. Now she could include fun *and* responsible on her list.

Our family of origin was likely lacking in good models for healthy, loving relationships, especially in conflict management. But our chosen relationships can be different if we educate ourselves about the ingredients of a successful relationship and then look for someone who values learning about these things too. Because my parents did not have a happy marriage, I needed that education, and John Gottman's work was extremely helpful.

Misplaced belief in "potential"

So many people are misled by what they believe is someone's *potential.* They believe their love or caring will bring out the other person's potential, and then the person will bloom like a giant sunflower in a bright sunny yard. My clients would say, "But maybe they *do* have potential. Should I give them more time? Maybe they will change. How can I know?"

The answer comes from asking a key question: Does the other person believe they need to change, not because you're upset with them, but because they genuinely see their responsibility and their part in the problem? Are they putting in the effort to alter their behavior? If they don't accept responsibility for mistakes or bad decisions and instead blame others (maybe even you), this is a giant red flag. *They aren't going to change no matter what you do, because they see nothing wrong with their behavior.* This may seem obvious, but it's easily missed and it's *the* critical predictor. Not taking responsibility is a hallmark of someone who will continue their unhealthy behavior. They will not change.

Many people ignore this fatal warning because they refuse to believe that some people don't change or grow. Instead, they think everyone deserves a second and third chance. Unfortunately, people are often naïve about how difficult it is to change, even when someone wants to. Think for a moment about how hard it is for you to change things about yourself, even when you are motivated.

If they do *not* take responsibility for their behavior, I can guarantee you that despite their occasional sincere apologies for their repeated unhealthy behavior, this should be all you need to decide to dissolve a relationship. It should elevate to a five-stage alarm if they become annoyed or fly into a rage when you try to talk with them about their behavior—even if tearful apologies follow. It's a RED ALERT. *Never* ignore this red flag. We need *to trust what we observe* and realize that what we see is often just the *tip of a massive iceberg.*

Too often, we stay in relationships long after we have become unhappy. We tell our friends, therapist, coworkers, and family all about what isn't working, focusing mainly on the failings or incompatibility of the other person. While a certain amount of this may be necessary to sort out our feelings, it's not what we should stay focused on. Instead, discuss your unhappiness with your partner or see a couple's therapist. Look at your own behavior and attitudes. What is your contribution? And if you continue to be unhappy, focus on what keeps you from leaving. There are many complicated situations involving children, finances, and fear of retaliation, to name a few. Focus on why you stay and what you can do to help yourself overcome those hurdles. The more you work on what you want and how you will make that happen, the more your time and energy will create the future you want. Focusing on what you don't want does not help you create a future you do want.

Luckily, we can learn many of the critical skills we need in choosing who we allow to be close to us in the first place. We can read books and articles, talk with others, and become educated and wise observers. Of course, it doesn't mean we won't occasionally make mistakes or choose poorly. But when relationships fail or our feelings are hurt, we can have compassion for how hard this is for us. And when we're inclined to think it's because of something defective in us, we can work to sort out the facts. Maybe we contributed, but we may not be the total cause.

We all deserve healthy, loving, honest, and generous relationships with partners, spouses, and friends. But when we find ourselves drawn to the unhealthy familiar, we can step back, see the patterns, and make different choices. It won't be easy, and we may have to go through some painful lessons before we choose differently.

Will you sometimes feel insecure about your worthiness? Sure. And it will lessen as you keep working at having loving people in your life. Feeling uncertain about how lovable you are is an example of the familiar shame-speak of "broken, damaged, and unworthy."

Now you are on to how shame works and where those false beliefs come from. You also have the tools to change these beliefs. If they come from an inner part, you know how to listen to their experiences (see the chapter on Befriending). As your parts are relieved of their burdens through your compassionate listening, the adult part of you can be in the driver seat of your relationship choices, much as actual parents can listen to their children and still be in charge. Little by little, all of you will know, "I am worthy of love," and you will show up as worthy.

———

Chapter Takeaways

1. We are drawn to familiar, even unhealthy relationship dynamics due to unconscious patterns rooted in our past. Recognizing these patterns is crucial for breaking free from them.

2. It is important to understand that we cannot change others or fix their emotional issues. They must take responsibility and do the hard work for their own healing.

3. We should never ignore red flags or underestimate the potential dangers of overlooking warning signs.

4. It is important to build a clear template of what we want based on positive experiences and preferences in our relationships rather than focusing on what we don't want or didn't like.

5. There are researched principles about what makes relationships work, and there are behaviors and attitudes that destroy them. You can learn them, and it is ideal if your relationship partner learns and practices them too.

Reflection Question

Who in your life makes you feel loved? What is it about the way they relate to you that feels so loving?

Practice

Got your notebook?

1. Identify a belief about yourself that you can see has been detrimental to finding healthy relationships. Examples may be, "People only love me because they need me." "Someone who is more together than I am would never love me." "I'll be friends with anyone who will befriend me."

2. What positive true phrase can you use to remind yourself to change that pattern? For example, if your pattern is accepting breadcrumbs, remind yourself: "Maybe I learned to make do with crumbs growing up, but I am worthy of loving attention, being listened to, and having my needs considered by anyone I am in relationship with."

3. Write down the positive statement you can use to counter a false belief you carry.

PART 3

FORGIVENESS

Introduction

To forgive is to set a prisoner free and discover that the prisoner was you."

- Lewis B. Smedes

When I started reading professional literature on forgiveness, I thought I had an adequate understanding, but as I got further into the texts and studies, I discovered I had a superficial understanding of the true meaning of forgiveness. My concept of forgiveness was barely beyond the Sunday School version. And I certainly didn't know about the research showing how forgiveness impacts our mental, emotional, and physical well-being. Those studies and my experiences have contributed to my belief in the power of forgiveness.

In the following pages, I want to introduce two writers who have studied and written about forgiveness extensively. Robert Enright is a psychologist and professor who has researched the psychological aspects of forgiveness. The second is the late Lewis Smedes, a renowned Christian author, theologian, and professor who has written extensively about forgiveness.

Enright is the founder of the International Forgiveness Institute and the Enright Process Model of Forgiveness. As an article in *Time* magazine said, "Dr. Forgiveness, as he's known, took forgiveness out of the confessional and transformed it into the subject of quantifiable research. In short, to forgive is no longer just divine." (*Time*, 1999) Through hundreds of science-based studies, Enright has found significant evidence that forgiveness has many positive outcomes—emotionally and physically. He has developed and researched a very clear forgiveness process. As one of his colleagues wrote on the International Forgiveness Institute website, "The research on forgiveness by Robert Enright and his colleagues may be as important to the treatment of emotional and mental disorders as the discovery of sulfa drugs and penicillin were to the treatment of infectious diseases."

Lewis Smedes taught at the Fuller Theological Seminary and was the author of fifteen books on forgiveness. Smedes' writings are straightforward and representative of a loving and accepting Christian perspective. If you'd like a fuller immersion in the forgiveness process, I hope you'll explore the work of these two men. See the Resource section for suggestions.

The Power of Forgiveness

Forgiveness may be the most neglected of all the healing arts.
—Lewis Smedes

"I can't even talk about forgiveness," Jennifer told me. "Just the word makes me mad. I'd have to call it something else, but even then, I just hate the thought of letting someone off the hook."

My client, Julie, had a similar reaction. She had talked many times about how bitter and resentful she was about being bullied throughout her school years. "I just wished I could not think about it so much," she said. But when I gently introduced the concept of forgiveness as a way to let go of the past, she said without hesitation, "What? I will never forgive anyone. Are you saying I should just forget and give them all a pass? I will never do that."

But does forgiveness require free passes or forgetting? There are a lot of misconceptions about forgiveness. In fact, since ancient times, disagreements abound about the definition of forgiveness, about who can forgive, and questions concerning the moral value of it. But let's sidestep these arguments and focus instead on the psychological and physical benefits for you of forgiving. As Jack Kornfield, a Buddhist teacher and psychologist said, "In Buddhist psychology, forgiveness is not a moral commandment but a way to end suffering, to bring dignity and harmony to our lives. It is a way to let go of the pain from the past."

What forgiveness is not

To dispel the many myths about forgiveness, I'll start with what forgiveness is *not* since these myths are major stumbling blocks to many. For example, if you think forgiving is giving someone a pass, you will be rankled at the idea. No one wants to give their transgressor a free pass. But as you'll see, forgiveness doesn't ask this of you. Nor is forgiveness about forgetting and denying your pain or humiliation. Instead, for our discussion, forgiveness is about letting the past become the past without forsaking yourself.

Forgiveness isn't the same as the shame response of appease–collapse–submit. Remember that your central nervous system initiates the shame response in situations of overwhelming fear and trauma. Forgiveness is a conscious choice.

Another common misunderstanding is that forgiveness is for the religious. As the Lord's Prayer entreats, "And forgive us our trespasses as we forgive those that trespass against us." Indeed, all religions teach that forgiveness is good for the forgiver, but belief in God isn't required for forgiveness to be of benefit.

Many wrongly believe that *not* forgiving the abuser or offender keeps them in a kind of emotional hell. However, we don't know if our lack of forgiving causes our offenders to suffer. For all we know, they're doing just fine, but our own experience shows that harboring resentment and anger while living in the past keeps us in our own personal hell. As Nelson Mandela said, "Resentment is like drinking poison and hoping it will kill your enemies." (Mandela 1995) Fortunately, the forgiveness we're exploring is a process that can lead us out of that hell without tolerating or minimizing the injustices we have suffered.

Forgiveness isn't as simple as saying, "I forgive you." It's a process, not a quick fix. By approaching it with small steps and then a few more, you'll find, as many have, that what seemed impossible is possible and life-altering. As Robert Enright wrote, "It is hard and sometimes painful work. Serious emotional wounds require serious medicine. People need to go through a process to understand their feelings, and they also need to take action." (Enright and Fitzgibbons 2015)

Does forgiveness mean putting up with offensive or abusive behavior? If you're in an abusive relationship, for example, does forgiving mean that you should continue in that relationship? Of course not. In his book, *Shame and Grace,* Lewis Smedes wrote, "Forgiving and tolerating have nothing in common. " (Smedes 1993)

If we forgive someone who has hurt us, does it leave us unprotected? For example, have you thought that if you forgive, you'll be more vulnerable to being hurt in the future? Cynthia certainly did. Her sister had bullied her as a kid. Then, years later, she had an affair with Cynthia's husband. "If I forgive her, she'll just hurt me again," Cynthia told me. "Hating her helps me keep up my guard. Someone must hold her accountable. I'm not going to be her punching bag, and I'm not going to pretend she never hurt me." She knew her sister was dangerous and responsible for a childhood of torture. But she was wrong to think that forgiveness would require that she put herself in harm's way or forget what her sister had done. Cynthia decided she would keep a safe distance from her sister. Forgiveness isn't about not holding someone accountable or failing to protect yourself.

What about the adage "forgive and forget"—the idea that forgiving means we're supposed to forget what our offender did to us? No, we don't forget. Forgiveness is necessary precisely because we haven't been able to forget. Forgiveness isn't a giant eraser, nor is it about denying or minimizing what happened to us. Instead, to forgive, we need to know what happened, how much it hurt us, and how we felt then. How else could we know what we're forgiving?

Forgiveness also isn't about making excuses for someone's behavior. Even if the offender was a wounded person, we must remember that not all wounded people hurt others. Instead, our offenders made a choice to do what they did, and even though they may not have intended to hurt us so deeply, they did hurt us. Forgiving is a way to free us from that wounding.

Forgiveness doesn't deny the reality that how we were treated has affected us. On the contrary, forgiveness is impossible until we own the painful truth that our injuries impacted our lives. This pain and the desire to heal and release the past is the most important motivation to consider forgiveness.

Making excuses

Sometimes, we make excuses for those who hurt us without realizing how this impedes our healing. This is especially true when the person who hurt us was our primary care-taker. I distinctly remember an incident when I was visiting my family from college. I had gone to a church service with my family where I met two of my mother's friends. When she introduced me, they were surprised that she had an older daughter. "Oh," they said to me, "we thought you must be her younger sister because she never told us she had an older daughter." I was hurt, but I tried to brush it off. Still, I couldn't understand why my mother had denied my existence to her friends.

Then, in my fifties, when I learned that she had conceived me "illegitimately," I told myself that her shame must have been so terrible that she rejected me. However, as I made my own forgiveness journey while writing this book, I had to face a painful truth. Not all mothers who conceive in shame reject their children. My mother chose to reject me, and as a result of her rejection, I learned to reject myself. That, in turn, interfered with my ability to trust that someone could love and cherish me and caused me decades of heartache.

Working through the forgiveness process, I realized that there were many layers to forgiving my mother. I wanted to forgive her for the rejection I experienced. Then I had to face the realization there was another layer of anger, devastating pain, and disappointment, because she wasn't able to stand up and protect me or her other children from my stepfather. But as I worked through the layers of forgiving, I suddenly remembered a time when she did stand up for me. It meant everything to me at the time and still does. It's interesting that I had lost that positive memory until I started peeling off the layers of my pain. Eventually, I found room in my heart to forgive and remember the good. Forgiving is often a process that unfolds in layers, and because my feelings about my mother, including my love for her, are complicated, the process is ongoing.

Is reconciliation required?

Does forgiveness require reconciliation? Do we need to allow our offenders into our lives? No. Forgiveness allows us to have the awareness and respect we deserve to protect ourselves and those we love. Forgiveness never asks us to be foolish or give up our rights for safety and respect.

Additionally, some mistakenly believe that forgiving someone requires informing the person that we've forgiven them and asking for an apology. Not so. The beauty of the forgiveness we're exploring is that we don't need anything from our offenders. We don't ever have to speak to them, and even if they're dead, it doesn't matter. Forgiveness doesn't require them to be present, and we certainly don't need an apology to forgive. This kind of forgiveness is for you, and it's between you and you.

What about legal recourse?

Forgiveness also doesn't mean you must give up the pursuit of justice. You can seek legal recourse if your offender has broken the law. Consider the example of Pope John Paul II, who was shot and wounded on a spring Sunday morning as he entered St. Peter's Square in 1986. The Sunday morning following the shooting, the Pope issued a recorded message from his hospital bed, asking people to pray for the man who pulled the trigger. Referring to his would-be assassin as "my brother," the Pope offered his "sincere forgiveness." However, when a reporter asked him how he could forgive the man who shot him and wounded three others, the Pope said, "One forgives in one's heart, in the sight of God, but the criminal still serves his time in Caesar's jail." Forgiveness never means surrendering justice.

Superheroes

Contrary to what some may think, forgiveness isn't something that only superheroes can do. Examples of ordinary people forgiving grave offenses can offer a glimpse into how they navigated the forgiveness process. An amazing example happened in 2006 in the Amish community of West Nickel Mines, Pennsylvania. On a Monday morning, when the kids were in their classroom, a deranged gunman with multiple weapons strapped to his body burst into the one-room school. He immediately ordered the boys and the two adult women to leave. He then tied up the girls. As the authorities arrived, he shot all ten girls, killing five before he killed himself.

Within hours of the tragic shooting, the community announced that they had forgiven the gunman, who was a non-Amish neighbor with a wife and several children. Still convulsing in shock and grief, some of the Amish took food to the gunman's widow. Six days later, having just buried their own murdered daughters, thirty Amish members attended the gunman's funeral and comforted his wife. In addition, as money poured in from around the world to the Amish community, they diverted the funds to the killer's family, even though many victims faced substantial medical bills themselves.

Hearing about this tragedy and the Amish community's forgiveness, we may wonder how such forgiveness was even possible in the face of such a devastating tragedy. We may be tempted to question the sincerity of their forgiveness, or we might think they were superhuman. However, in *Amish Grace: How Forgiveness Transcended Tragedy* (Kraybill, Nolt and Weaver-Zercher 2010), the authors discuss how Amish communities cultivate forgiveness as a daily practice. Forgiveness is an essential principle of their religion. Their well-practiced forgiveness helped them transform their anguish. They had "forgiving-fit hearts" from a lifetime of practice.

Their forgiveness wasn't just a one-time decision. In a newspaper article commemorating the tenth anniversary of "the happening," as it was referred to, one of the Amish members told a reporter for *The Guardian*, "Everyone is doing pretty well, for the best part. But we still wonder: why did it happen?" And despite the Amish's legendary powers of forgiveness, he said, it was a struggle to stay constant. "You have to fight the bitter thoughts."

From these comments and those of the parents who lost their daughters, it's clear that the decision by the community to forgive the killer wasn't as simple as it may have seemed. "It's not a once-and-done thing," said an Amish mother. "It is a lifelong process." Another parent added, "The heartache is still there. I take one day at a time."

An Amish father who lost a daughter told the reporter that even when the decision to forgive is made, "it takes a while for each person's emotions to catch up with such an outward decision." On the day of the shooting, when he saw the wounded girls fighting for their lives in the hospital, he admitted how angry he was. The Amish did not want to be considered saintly or "stoically stuffing their feelings into a box." No. They acknowledged their feelings and worked to accept their thoughts and feelings of anger and hate, but their forgiveness didn't require giving up justice. As several community members told *The Guardian* reporter, if the gunman had lived, they would have wanted justice—not the death penalty, but justice.

The Amish community knew forgiveness offered them a healing balm for their unimaginable pain. "Forgiveness is the one good thing that can come out of this tragedy," said a grieving father. With the shooter dead, he said, there was nowhere for the anger to go, and the Amish believe that harboring anger and resentment is corrosive. "It will eat you up. Forgiveness," he said, "is so ingrained in our heritage that it's part of our character." Again, it isn't about denying feelings. They could have held onto bitterness, hatred, anger, and anguish. Instead, they mastered the repeated practice of forgiveness. But like any of us, they had to work at it even after their initial offering to forgive.

Yes, this tragedy is an extreme example of forgiveness, but what lessons can we take from the Amish? They weren't superhuman. One day at a time, they diligently practice remaining steadfast to their commitment to forgive the man who murdered their daughters. They acknowledged the hateful thoughts that arose from their grief and didn't allow their anger to inhibit them from continuing their forgiveness practice. They didn't hesitate to offer forgiveness, because they were clear about what it entails and didn't question the power and healing it brings.

The outcome of forgiving our offenders is also *our* emotional healing. Smedes writes, "We are not responsible for what other people did to us, but we are responsible for what we do with what happened to us." The science behind forgiveness shows that we can experience varying degrees of emotional healing by forgiving our offenders. For many who have suffered grave injustices, forgiving is a herculean accomplishment, but it doesn't require superhuman powers.

———

Chapter Takeaways

1.   Forgiveness is not about letting someone off the hook or forgetting the past. It is about freeing ourselves from the burden of resentment and anger. It is a way to end our own suffering.
2.   Forgiveness is a process, not a quick fix.
3.   Forgiveness does not require reconciliation or allowing offenders back into our lives, especially if they exhibit harmful behavior.
4.   Forgiveness is not reserved for superheroes or those with extraordinary abilities. It's a practice that anyone can cultivate over time, one day at a time.

Reflection Question

What was the attitude of your family toward forgiveness?

Practice

Notebook at the ready:

Choose one of the misconceptions mentioned in the text that particularly resonates with you or challenges your beliefs.

- Forgiveness means giving someone a free pass.
- Forgiveness requires reconciliation.
- The process of forgiveness is forgive and forget.
- Forgiveness means we are denying we were hurt.
- If we forgive, we are more vulnerable.
- Forgiving means we put up with offensive or abusive behavior.
- If we forgive, we shouldn't seek legal recourse.
- True forgiveness means we never have a negative or hateful thought toward our offender.
- Only superheroes can truly forgive.

By clarifying this as a misconception, how might it affect your future approach to forgiveness?

18

What Is Forgiveness?

Forgiveness is the greatest gift you can give yourself. It is not for the other person.

—Maya Angelou

M y friend, Rachel, and I were enjoying an early breakfast when the subject of forgiveness came up. As I shared some of the insights I was gaining from researching the subject, she told me about the biggest "aha!" moment she'd had about forgiveness. Years earlier, she told me, a therapist had said that forgiving someone who had deeply hurt her didn't mean she had to forget. This information made all the difference, she said.

Rachel was going that day to visit her father's gravesite. It would be the first time since his death. She loved her father but had many unresolved disappointments and hurt feelings when he died. She had no expectations and wasn't thinking about forgiveness when she walked through the cemetery looking for his gravesite. But when she arrived at his tombstone and read the inscription, "With humility and God's grace, he did his level best," she paused and thought that perhaps he did do his best. Spontaneously, she decided that she would accept this as true, even though many of his choices had been emotionally painful and troubling to her.

But what happened next truly surprised her. Suddenly, Rachel told me that a wave of energy swept over her, and almost simultaneously, she felt a huge weight leaving her body. She sensed relief and lightness. "I guess that is what forgiveness can feel like," she said. "But I wonder if this would have happened if we hadn't discussed forgiveness earlier." Perhaps bringing forgiveness into her awareness by talking about it allowed her to let go of the pain her expectations had created by wanting her father to be different. Finally, she could acknowledge with compassion, "He did his level best."

We may still ask ourselves, however, "Why forgive?" Isn't forgiveness like appeasing someone? No. Forgiveness is something we do for ourselves. One big reason to forgive is that the burden of the resentments and anger we carry with us has become too much. We want relief. The pain of the injustices may no longer be like a hot knife in our back and more like a smoldering ember, but it's still alive in us, ready to burst into flame with the mention of a name or the flash of a memory. We want release from our painful past. We want the injustices to be over with. As one writer said, "Forgiving releases you from the punishment of a self-made prison in which you are both the inmate and the jailor." (Childre and Martin 1999)

As we further consider the process and benefits of forgiveness, we might wonder whether we should forgive only those who deserve it or only those who show remorse. Quite the opposite. As Robert Enright said, "Forgiveness is a *gift* we give to those who have hurt us. It is a gift because it is *not* something they earned." (Enright 2001) Forgiveness is a merciful response to the injustices of lack of respect, kindness, generosity, fairness, and love. You offer this gift to them *despite* what they have done to you.

Giving up revenge

Most of us don't start the forgiveness process by wanting to give a gift to those who have hurt us—quite the opposite. Our disdain and disgust for our offenders can feel like self-respect. Even our culture supports and encourages us to see them as subhuman. We talk to our friends on social media and in casual conversation about how callous they are. These are our battle stories in which we were gravely wounded. We want others to know what we went through, so we're reluctant to let go of our stories.

Gradually, however, we recognize that our anger and revenge fantasies haven't made things better or fairer for us. Still, many people feel they have the right to get even.

Forgiveness asks us to surrender our need for revenge. It means giving up our fantasies of our offenders suffering terrible humiliation and a lifelong tortured mind. To forgive means we stop trying to hurt or discredit our offenders by telling our abuse stories, dragging their names through the mud, or making snide comments. We also don't snub or act rudely toward them if we encounter them. This is a big ask, isn't it? But healing our suffering requires something big, and forgiveness is big—especially in a culture that promotes revenge.

My client, Virginia, hated her ex-husband. She was haunted for decades by the emotional pain and humiliation she felt and the cruel ways he treated their two boys while they were in his custody. She blamed her ex for robbing her of the joy of young motherhood and was convinced that his mistreatment of their boys had caused them psychological suffering. Yet, that was twenty years earlier.

During one of our sessions, she fantasized aloud about how she would like to kill him. "At least I'd go to prison feeling satisfied," she said. Then she caught herself. "But killing him won't make up for what my boys suffered or how helpless and heartbroken I felt." Virginia wanted relief from the painful burden she'd carried for two decades. While forgiveness wouldn't balance the scales of the past, it was the only way to heal the corrosive poison of resentment she continued to carry.

But when I mentioned forgiveness to her, she felt betrayed. "How can you even mention that?" she asked. "How's that going to help anything?" Virginia didn't yet understand that the benefits of forgiveness were for herself, not for her ex.

Healing the past by healing the now

How can forgiveness help heal the shame-wounding that happened in our past? Our healing is not in the past. It is in the present, and the wounding that needs healing is how we feel about ourselves in the here and now. Too often, we label ourselves by what our offenders did and said to us: "I'm an incest survivor," "I was an unwanted child," "I was emotionally abused," or "I'm stupid." Remember that as children, we accepted what our caregivers and teachers told us as truth. Even as adults, if we're repeatedly told that we're worthless, lazy, or unworthy, we come to accept those labels over time as valid. But forgiveness invites us to see ourselves and potentially even our perpetrators differently. We're much more than anything that has happened to us, and forgiveness allows us to be free of the limiting false beliefs we were taught.

You'll see in the following pages that as we forgive, we find a strength we didn't know we had. We find we're stronger than our wounding—bruised but not broken. We no longer need to be trapped in the anger and resentment of our past. Enright wrote, "Forgiveness reduces anger in people treated unjustly by others, and as the anger decreases, psychological well-being is enhanced." Stress hormones that cause disease and early aging decrease. In some cases, symptoms of depression and anxiety resolve. Enright also said, "The more hurt you have incurred, the more important it is to forgive, at least for the purpose of your experiencing emotional healing." (Enright 2001)

Scientific studies of forgiving

No one has conducted more scientific research on the emotional-psychological benefits of forgiveness than Robert Enright, whom I introduced earlier as the founder of the International Forgiveness Institute and the author of hundreds of studies about forgiveness.

His research includes incest survivors, people in drug rehabilitation, dying people in hospice, and abused women in shelters. He has also studied heart attack patients in cardiac units of hospitals, bullying issues in schools, and civilians in other countries suffering from the tragedies and scars of war.

As you read about the men and women in his studies, I trust their stories will inspire hope that forgiveness can give you a chance at a healthier and happier future as well.

Enright's study of incest survivors particularly moved me. Betrayal and sexual violation by a family member are among the cruelest offenses. When Enright and his colleague began interviewing twelve incest survivors as potential candidates for their forgiveness study, no one was surprised when every one of the women said they would *never* forgive their perpetrator. The women thought this admission would exclude them from the study, but instead, Enright and colleague Suzanne Freedman deemed them perfect candidates.

The women were from a Midwestern city, all were Caucasian, and they ranged in age from twenty-four to fifty-four. All reported that they were sexually abused as children: fifty percent by their biological father, eight percent by a stepfather, sixteen percent by a brother, twelve percent by a grandfather, and eight percent by an uncle. Three were married, four were divorced, and five were single. Some had full-time careers, and several were college students. One worked part time, and several worked and went to college.

Each woman took a battery of psychological tests before the study, which measured anxiety, depression, self-esteem, and hope. Enright noted, "All were anxious, depressed, and suffered low self-esteem." He then randomly divided the women into two groupings of six each, and they all met weekly for fourteen months. (Enright and Fitzgibbons 2015)

One group met together and individually with an educator (not a counselor) trained in Enright's forgiveness process. Each of the women received a manual similar to the book by Enright, *Forgiveness Is a Choice* (Enright 2001), which describes the forgiveness process used in their sessions. This is a similar process to what you'll learn in the next chapter.

In addition, after the study started, each woman periodically filled out a questionnaire asking them to rate their feelings about their perpetrator. This questionnaire was administered to assess progress at periodic intervals.

In the other group, the six women participated in weekly individual counseling with a licensed *counselor* but were not exposed to any education or discussion about forgiveness.

After fourteen months, the six women in the forgiveness training group took the same battery of tests they had taken before the study. Each showed a *noteworthy decrease* in anxiety and *no* clinical signs of depression. In addition, they reported feeling more hopeful about their future. Enright wrote, "What is interesting is that participants do not have to score exceptionally high on the forgiveness scale to realize considerable psychological improvement in hope, anxiety, and depression."

The six women who had not received any forgiveness training also re-took the original battery of tests. Their results indicated they remained depressed and anxious. Their post-study results showed no change. Enright and his group then enrolled these six women in a program similar to the one their cohorts had experienced. Post-study, they too showed improvement in anxiety and depression.

All twelve women had additional benefits. They discovered a new sense of their own strengths and courage in the process of forgiving. Enright and Richard Fitzgibbons wrote, "They realize now that they are stronger than any injustices that can ever be thrown at them by others. They can confidently meet the future, knowing they have learned and embraced a scientifically supported antidote to cruelty: forgiveness." Reflecting on his study and the scientific literature available to therapists, Enright further observed, "No other treatment program for incest survivors has, to our knowledge, produced such positive results." (Enright and Fitzgibbons 2015)

In another study, Enright gave a battery of psychological tests to fourteen men and women in an inpatient treatment facility for drug addiction. All had noteworthy depression and anxiety. Like the incest group, they were divided into two groups, with one group focusing on forgiving someone who had significantly hurt them and going through the protocol of the inpatient treatment program. The second group went through the drug treatment program protocol without exposure to forgiveness.

At the end of six weeks, when each patient took a posttest, the group that engaged in the forgiveness practice had less anxiety, anger, and vulnerability to drug use and increased forgiveness and self-esteem. Moreover, like the women in the incest group, the forgiveness-focused group went from considerable depression to no depression, which remained valid at the four-month follow-up. The other group decreased in depression but remained clinically depressed.

In another example of the power of forgiveness, Enright's team selected seventeen men with coronary artery disease treated in the cardiac unit for a study. All participants confirmed they could remember a specific incident of being treated so unjustly that just thinking about it made them angry. Participants were asked to reflect on and discuss the unjust incident in detail. Then, they were administered tests that measured anger and myocardial perfusion. Myocardial perfusion is an imaging test, also called a nuclear stress test, used to assess how well the heart functions by measuring blood flow through the heart muscle. These seventeen men were then randomly divided into two groups. One group was given the book, *Forgiveness Is a Choice* and met weekly with a psychologist for ten weeks. The other group was taught coping strategies for life stressors without any deliberate intent to reduce anger and no mention of forgiveness.

Participants in the forgiveness group showed a significant increase in the degree of forgiveness compared to the other group. And "those in the forgiveness group also demonstrated a significant reduction in anger," according to the researchers. But the forgiveness group also showed a significant positive change in their blood flow. According to Enright, this study suggests that "forgiveness therapy has a statistically significant effect on a major organ of the body."

As positive as all of these studies are, we must not assume that forgiving means we'll be free of depression or anxiety. Everyone is different, and your outcome may vary. But even if your improvement is only a little bit, isn't that better than no improvement at all? As Enright says, "If you have tried a variety of techniques to help you attain an inner quiet but are still emotionally jumbled and uneasy, perhaps it is time to consider forgiveness." (Enright and Fitzgibbons 2015)

Minimizing our wounds

Sometimes, we think forgiveness is unnecessary because we feel there isn't much to forgive. Maybe we want to protect ourselves from feeling how deeply hurt we were by our mother, father, or family member. "Others had it much worse," we might say. "I'm okay now, so it doesn't really matter. It wasn't that bad. I'm still standing."

Alternatively, we may displace our pain. For example, instead of accepting that the wounds inflicted by our mother cut the deepest, we focus on how terrible our stepfather was, as I did. Or we blame ourselves: "I was a difficult kid. No wonder my mother didn't stick up for me. I caused her so much grief," we might say.

But when we look more closely, we find that we have indeed been deeply hurt, and dismissing, diminishing, or comparing our wounds to another's is disrespectful to ourselves. Statements to ourselves, such as "stop being a baby," "man up," "others are way worse off than you are," or "I had it much worse than you" are dismissive and disrespect our pain and suffering.

Often, we don't connect our feelings of anxiety, anger, depression, and low self-esteem to the fact that we carry and sometimes nurse our resentment. We blame our emotional distress on the injustices we have experienced. But as we learn to forgive, we become aware that we have the choice to surrender our "right" to revenge, hatred, and resentment. We can stop dragging our offender's name through the mud, and we will free up our energy as we do.

Hate and resentment take energy and keep us stuck in the past. We want a different future from our past. Forgiveness is something we can offer to another human being, so *we* can be free to create the life we want. Smedes put it this way, "Forgiveness is the only way to free ourselves from the trap of persistent and unfair pain." (Smedes 1997)

Forgiveness also spares others from the effects of your bitterness and resentments. I cared about an uncle of mine, but I still avoided him because his conversations were too often rants about how other relatives had harmed him many years ago. As a young adult, I saw how much energy this resentment consumed and how others avoided him also.

The journey of forgiveness is a journey from the known to the unknown. It is not easy or familiar. Still, it will allow you the opportunity to see and feel differently about yourself and the circumstances that created such heartache and suffering.

Let's take a closer look at the forgiveness process. As Mahatma Gandhi declared, "Forgiveness is the attribute of the strong." (Gandhi 1995) We get stronger as we forgive. The steps in the next chapter are similar to the ones that Enright's study participants followed.

———

Chapter Takeaways

1. Forgiveness means surrendering our "right" to revenge. Forgiveness is especially important in our culture, which often promotes revenge.
2. Forgiveness is not about healing the past. It's about healing our present. It involves challenging the false beliefs and labels we've accepted about ourselves due to past traumas.
3. Scientific studies, particularly by Robert Enright, demonstrate the psychological and physiological benefits of forgiveness. It can lead to reduced anxiety and depression, increased self-esteem, and a desire to use our suffering to help others.
4. Sometimes, we downplay our pain or compare our suffering to others, dismissing the need for

forgiveness. However, it's crucial to recognize and respect our own wounds and not diminish our experiences.

Reflection Question

Have your beliefs about forgiveness shifted after reading the scientific studies included in this chapter?

Practice

Notebook ready:
1. Giving up revenge thoughts and stopping ourselves from talking disparaging about our offenders can be challenging. Identify one person in your life who you are willing to release from your revenge fantasies.
2. Now notice and congratulate yourself every time you stop yourself in the future from maligning this person.
3. Why did you want to give up your revenge thoughts?

19

Forgiveness as a Process

Forgiveness can save your life. No one wants to waste time when it comes to our healing. Forgiveness is strong medicine.

—Robert Enright

The women in Enright's incest group were confident they would never forgive their abusers when they started. So how did those women end up forgiving those who had hurt them so badly? First, they decided to *begin* the process and then they continued the work despite their painful and confusing feelings.

All forgiveness begins with an intention. And then a first step. It is not a straight path and there are many obstacles— the swamp of resentments, the hills that appears too steep, and the journey too long. This is a journey of courage and it can sometimes seem as painful as the original injury. Why risk this pain? What is your motivation? Stop for a moment and reflect on your motivation. What is it? After years of carrying the burden of your anger and resentment, perhaps you're ready to be done with it. How can you reclaim your life in the present if your thoughts are in the past? You can't.

Even as you begin the process, there will be times when you will hesitate and old patterns will creep back in— Recommit. And then recommit again.

Phase 1: Who has unjustly hurt you?

We begin our forgiveness journey by asking ourselves who has hurt us. This question may seem obvious, but Enright encourages us to list those we believe have harmed us and those we continue to feel resentment and anger towards. As you list names, more people may come to mind. You can add it to your list as you do this work.

Now, take a look at your list. Does anything about it surprise you? Is it longer or shorter than you imagined? Did you write it relatively quickly, or did you hesitate to add a particular person or feel your anger rise when you thought of someone? Either way, simply notice what comes up for you.

If your childhood was a painful collage of betrayal and pain, you might feel significant anguish by just naming your oppressors and abusers. If you feel too overwhelmed, I encourage you to pause and consider working with a counselor or therapist who can guide you in your healing.

If the therapist you choose isn't trained or familiar with a forgiveness process, you can always return to this text or one of Enright's or Smedes' publications when you feel the timing is right. You could also tell your therapist about these resources. They may appreciate knowing about the science behind forgiveness. Above all, know that reaching out shows strength and self-respect.

When you're ready to begin, decide who you will forgive first. Gauge your choice on how emotionally strong you feel. For me, I started with people whose painful treatment gnawed at me the most. Still, I found that my forgiveness process had layers.

For example, I started with someone I had felt resentment toward since I was nine—my stepfather. Only later did I realize that I had focused on him because facing the pain that had cut the deepest was too difficult—the wounding of my mother's rejection. I was surprised to discover how much pain I still carried from her failure to emotionally bond with me.

We may feel disloyal as we pull off our blinders and see how our parents or others we trusted were emotionally insensitive, abusive, or neglectful. But this is not a healthy loyalty. Part of being an adult is to face the reality of our childhood—to take a good clear look at what happened, who was involved, and how it hurt us, and then decide what we want to do about it.

Patricia was incensed as she told me how her husband had accused her of intentionally bad-mouthing him at a family gathering. "How can he think that of me? I would never do that to him. Doesn't he know who I am? This crosses the line. I will never forgive him." For weeks, Patricia hung onto her anger. As she did, she remembered other times when her husband accused her of things she thought were unfair—even cruel. This infuriated her even more. No doubt, Patricia's husband's accusations had hurt her. Still, when we're intensely reactive, angry, or deeply insulted about something, it's often because it scrapes off the scab of a former unhealed wounding. Intense feelings from unhealed wounds are easily triggered.

In Patricia's situation, her mother frequently and unfairly accused her of lying and purposefully causing trouble in the family. If Patricia had only focused on her husband's painful accusations, she wouldn't have become aware, nor faced the deep wounding of her mother's allegations and emotional betrayal. Her mother's wounding had been the most painful, making it very difficult for Patricia to face. So, she initially focused on her husband's accusations, only later realizing his accusations mirrored childhood interactions with her mother.

What are you forgiving?

You may think you're forgiving your father for beating you or your mother for never loving you. And that may be true, but the wounding you experienced has consequences far beyond the abuse itself. A big part of your wounding is what you were falsely taught about yourself and came to believe was true. Ask yourself: Did you believe you were broken, unlovable, and not good enough because of how you were treated? Most of us did. Did those feelings and beliefs affect your choices of friends and romantic partners? Did it affect your educational or career choices or how you treated yourself? This is the focus of forgiveness.

Were you blamed for your oppressor's abusive behavior? Rest assured; abuse is never the child's fault. All children misbehave, talk back to their parents, break things, lose things, tell lies, and push boundaries. But none of those behaviors deserve abuse—being yelled at, being spanked, being beaten, slapped, verbally humiliated, demeaned, or punished for days is abuse. Likewise, a child is never responsible for sexual abuse, no matter how flirtatious, cuddly, wanting to be physically close, or curious about another's body.

Still, you may feel responsible for your abuse. Sadly, this is very common. It's also common for predators to tell you the abuse is your fault. For example, when I became sexually involved with a woman eighteen years my senior, I honestly thought I was to blame for initiating it. I was fifteen, and while I was a hormonal adolescent, I wasn't focused on sex. Nonetheless, there I was, and I believed I was to blame.

I wrestled with confusion about this relationship for decades—was she a molester or a sweetheart? Was I responsible? Then one day, when I was well into middle age, I told a friend about my history, and she asked me, "Did you want sex?" Suddenly, I remembered the first time she approached me sexually. I didn't want sex. I felt disgusted and remembered thinking, "What is she doing?" Friendship was all I wanted.

This short conversation with my friend was transformational. I no longer thought it was my fault. As I tried on this insight, I felt a wave of relief wash over me. It felt profoundly true. I wasn't to blame. I wasn't a bad girl. As Enright said, "Forgiveness matters primarily because it can reverse all of the lies you might believe about yourself." (Enright 2015)

To forgive or not

I will never forget my client, Lu, and what she modeled for me about forgiveness. She grew up with her mother and a much younger brother in the Bronx. Her mother began pimping her out for money as early as she could remember.

Sometimes it was with the superintendent of the housing project when her mother was behind in the rent. Sometimes it was with the grocer on the corner when they needed milk and bread. Other times, it was with men she didn't know. "I was a piece of meat. No one cared," she told me. Her wounding and betrayal were the worst I had ever encountered.

For months, Lu and I worked on healing her horrific pain of betrayal and dehumanization. Sometimes the cruelty she endured as a child and an adult overwhelmed me. Other clients told me horrible stories of rape, abuse, imprisonment, and child pornography rings—but all at the hands of fathers or stepfathers. This was her mother! I was shaken to my core as I tried to imagine how a mother could abuse and pimp out her own little daughter.

Gradually Lu's life began to improve. She met a roommate with a sweet little dog, and together they adopted another. Occasionally, the roommate joined us for a session with the dogs in tow. The roommate always came to discuss choices Lu was making that concerned her. Although Lu would act annoyed, I knew she appreciated the caring.

And then, one day, Lu came in, sat on the side of the sofa where she had always sat, and told me she wanted to *forgive* her mother. I was stunned. My first thoughts were, "Forgive her? Are you nuts? I'm nowhere near finished hating her!" I was shocked at my reaction—which I kept to myself—but it was how I felt. Then Lu told me, "I want to be free of her. I want it over."

Years later as I was going through my own forgiveness process, I would reflect on Lu and think if she could forgive, and if the incest survivors in Enright's study could forgive, if the Amish community could forgive, I could surely forgive.

I'm still in touch with Lu. It has been at least twenty-five years since we sat together in my office, and she showed me what it meant to forgive. I will forever be touched by her courage and grateful for her example.

Even after Lu's example, I wasn't proactive with clients about the concept of forgiveness. I would wait for them to broach the topic. I was sorting out my own misconceptions and didn't have a clear process. Now, I know that if I wait for a client to initiate exploring forgiveness, it may not happen on my watch. I bring it up gently, but confidently, because I know the power of forgiveness to heal even the worst of cruelties.

Phase 2: Are your offenders more than their cruel behavior?

When we reduce our offenders to the acts they have committed, we think of them as two-dimensional caricatures. My Uncle the Pervert. My Heartless Mother. My Nasty Grandfather. My Dad, the Mean Bastard Drunk. We don't have to feel anything toward them except disgust or contempt as long as we keep them in these boxes. "We shrink him (or her) to the size of what they did to us; they become the wrong they did to us," writes Smedes. "As a result, we're left with a two-dimensional image of who they are. They're no longer a confusing mixture of good and evil. But as we restore their humanity through forgiveness and compassion, we begin to see a real person, a botched self, no doubt, a hodgepodge of meanness and decency, lies and truths, good and evil." (Smedes 1993)

As one friend explained to me about her father, who had been abusive to her, "When my dad was good, fun, happy,

I loved him and felt like I wanted to be with him. He would take us to Disneyland, and he was completely different. When he was 'bad dad,' I was terrified and hated him. But he wasn't always 'bad dad' or any other labels."

Part of adulthood is realizing that no one is all bad or all good. We don't forget how they hurt us; instead, we add dimension to our understanding of them. We know our offenders didn't come into life as molesters or abusers. And people don't become parents intending to hurt, abuse, and humiliate their children. Instead, some horrible circumstances in their own lives taught them false beliefs about themselves, and they acted on those false beliefs and lies about themselves and others. Their empathy was thwarted. They lost contact with the wisdom of their hearts. But make no mistake—we aren't looking to condone their hurtful actions. Through the process of forgiveness, we try to see that they are more than what they did to us, and *we* are more than what they did to us.

It isn't enough to think, "I forgive you, you completely disgusting human." Why? Because all human beings have value. And forgiveness involves a change of *heart* toward our abusers and offenders. Part of the forgiving process consists in seeing the ones who hurt us as multidimensional human beings with *worth*. We can also have compassion for their learned behavior as we discover what happened to them and how patterns of abuse go for generations—until someone stops the pattern. We can have compassion for their life experiences. Some who behave violently and cruelly suffer from mental illness. People do not choose or catch mental illness. Some very terrible things happened to them, and as a result, they became sick. But we are not condoning their behavior.

We endeavor to see them as whole human beings who, *despite* what they did, are more than their worst behavior. In so doing, we also make room to *see ourselves as more than our worst behaviors*. As we look at self-forgiveness in an upcoming chapter, we can change our hearts toward ourselves and accept that we are all part of a fallible, sometimes thoughtless, sometimes even cruel humanity. Gradually, as we work through this phase of forgiveness, "we *feel* him (the offender) differently because we are making an attempt to *see* him differently." Smedes (1997) Perhaps it helps to remember again that nothing comes from heaven broken. Everyone comes into life loving and lovable.

Seeing our offenders as real people

How can we possibly see our offenders differently? Enright suggests we begin by imagining them as children. We can try to imagine this even if we don't know details about their childhood. This can change our perspective of anger and judgment that keeps us imprisoned and stuck in the past to one of compassion, understanding, and even empathy.

When I asked myself to imagine my stepfather as a child, I heard a clear voice in my head say, "I don't want to." It felt like my heart slammed shut. He had been the chief villain in my story, and I didn't want to let go of that storyline. But I also knew that keeping him in the villain role kept me in the victim role and stuck in the past.

I made myself remember the scant things I knew. Coming from a family with six children, he was second to last. His mother worked outside the home as a waitress to supplement her sickly husband's meager wages. As a boy, my stepfather raised and sold carrier pigeons to help buy food for himself and the family. Food was scarce; no one got all they wanted to eat. Dinnertime was always tense in his family. He once told me that if his father thought he had taken too much food, he would get backhanded so hard that it knocked him off his chair.

I tried to hold these stories in my mind, adding more to his story as I remembered bits and pieces of what he or his relatives had shared. Then, several years ago, my cousin compiled a family history. There I learned that during the early part of his life, my stepfather's family lived in caves or abandoned railroad cars. It was a life of hardship, toil, and never getting ahead.

This is how my stepfather grew up. For him, joining the military seemed a good choice despite the wars. He never spoke of his military experiences except to say the winters in Korea were bitterly cold and that he saved some of his rations to give to the Korean children who would beg him and the other Marines for food.

As a young father without healthy modeling about how to be a parent, his military experience was his parenting model. That was the best he could do. As I reflected on the bigger picture of who he was, I saw him in a broader context, and my contempt for him began to soften. I remembered the kind and generous things he did for me—the times of playing catch, the fishing trips, and the little soapbox car he built for me. Of course, I haven't forgotten the emotional abuse, but now when I think about him, I remember these good things, too. My heart doesn't just slam shut, and I'm not angry or resentful, just sad—for both of us.

Stopping the cycle through forgiveness

As we actively choose forgiving, we're modeling for our children and others a way to deal with the injustices of life besides anger, hate, and resentment. The International Forgiveness Institute points out, "We do not know how far-reaching our decisions to forgive may extend." After a quarter century of studying the moral virtue of forgiveness, Dr. Enright has become convinced that forgiveness is the missing piece to the peace puzzle. Over a dozen social scientific studies demonstrate that as people forgive, they become less angry, depressed, anxious, and more hopeful of their future. In other words, people become more peaceful within themselves, making the possibility of peace with others more likely. "And as you forgive, you give yourself a second chance at a beautiful life regardless of what happened to you." (Enright 2001) "The practice of forgiveness is our most important contribution to healing the world." (Williamson 2004)

How do you know if you're forgiving?

Does forgiveness mean we never have bitter or angry thoughts toward our offenders? No. As Smedes' wrote, "Sometimes people wonder how they could forgive someone they are still angry with. My response is: If you feel angry about what happened to you, congratulate yourself. Your anger is a clear sign that you are in touch with reality." (Smedes 1997) Remember the Amish parents who talked about not accepting angry thoughts? Instead, they acknowledged the emotions that came up and surrendered them, choosing forgiveness instead, no matter how often the anger arose. I found this insight particularly helpful as somehow, I thought that having angry or resentful thoughts about my offenders indicated that I was not forgiving them. Now I understand that the mind will have old resentments and angry, even revengeful thoughts, but we can choose whether we will feed those thoughts and feelings or whether we will choose to not let them stop our intention to forgive. The Amish were committed to forgiveness more than anything else, and when the anger arose, they focused on the forgiveness process. We have that choice also and not just for religious reasons, although that can be a sustaining support, but because we want to feel better. The pain and anguish we experienced from our offenders' behavior happened in the past, but the feelings stay alive in the present especially when we recall and retell our experiences. Forgiveness gives us the path to move beyond feelings and thoughts, not because they didn't happen or they weren't that bad, but because we want a future that is not filled with pain from the past.

As we make our forgiveness journey, it helps to have markers along the way. One marker is that you have committed to begin the process with a specific offender in mind. Another marker is being dedicated to surrendering your right or desire for revenge. Finally, even if you take steps backward, like making a snide comment or beginning a defaming story, you can stop, notice, and recognize the pattern. Then, you can choose to commit again to continuing your forgiveness journey. Relapses are to be expected. We may feel a deeper anger and thoughts of revenge for someone we thought we had forgiven. This is to be expected. What can you do? Practice the same steps you used in the past. Forgiving serious injuries requires time. Even for the religious who have asked for God's help to forgive, it is a process that requires focused intent and patience.

Remember that the incest survivors in Enright's study were still working to forgive after months into the forgiveness process. As Enright noted, if you had asked any of the women in the incest group to assess her progress in the fifth month or the eighth month, they would have concluded they weren't there yet and may even have doubted they would ever experience the forgiveness they were searching for. Forgiving grave wounding takes time, courage, and support.

Another marker much further down the path is that you don't feel disturbed or reactive when you hear the offender's name, think of them, or see them. Your skin no longer crawls, and your heart no longer races. You feel emotionally neutral.

Many people believe this neutrality is enough. While it isn't contempt, it isn't compassion or empathy either. Before I researched forgiveness, I thought neutrality was the end goal. But I also knew that neutrality didn't help me feel emotionally or physically complete. Just neutral. That changed, however, when I went through the forgiveness steps and saw my stepfather not as the man I judged as emotionally limited, cruel, and angry but as a wounded, unhealed, yet whole human being. When that happened, I found compassion and empathy for him. I felt the empathic barrier covering my heart melt, which felt healing.

I was particularly aware of this recently when, while having lunch with my elderly uncle, he began to talk about what a jerk my stepfather had been. Without thinking about it, I wanted to defend my stepfather, so I started telling my uncle about his upbringing. After I finished a brief summary, I said, "He acted like a jerk and even worse, but he wasn't that way for no reason. And his behavior didn't define him. He was more than his behavior, so I have forgiven him." My uncle has not brought up negative things about my stepfather since.

You may never feel those compassionate feelings for your abuser, and you may never want to. That's fine. Although some would disagree, there's no right or wrong way to forgive. You may go back and forth. You may think you've forgiven and then more feelings or memories surface. Forgiving grave injustices often takes years. Maybe a lifetime. But the process itself is healing. You may forgive to the point of feeling neutral about your offender, which may be enough for you. That's perfectly fine.

The combination of compassion and forgiveness is powerful medicine. It's the place of *our* inner peace. It may take some time to arrive at that juncture, but I hope that you give it a try. This means you won't stop until you can see a spark of compassion for all who have hurt you, even your abusers, as well as all who will hurt and offend you in the future.

At the very least, I hope you make forgiving a way of life. Forgiving is hard. No one in our culture finds it easy but if you have committed to the process, even if you lose your way and need to refocus, just by beginning "you are forgiving and should give yourself credit." (Enright 2001) Forgive the driver who cuts you off in traffic. Forgive the owner of the dog that poops on your lawn, every day. Forgive the family member who is irritating and talks constantly about themselves. Forgive the co-worker who doesn't pull their weight, or the political figures that lie and create false news. Forgive everything and everyone as soon as you can. Why? So, you don't carry resentment, unhappiness, rage and bitterness along with you. Aim to carry compassion, peace, and happiness instead. And if you can't find those feelings, ask yourself what is getting in the way. Almost every time you will find a resentment you carry about someone. You can always rededicate yourself to forgiveness.

Chapter Takeaways

1. Forgiveness is a process that can lead to personal transformation.
2. We begin the forgiveness process by identifying who has unjustly hurt us.
3. Next, we identify what we are forgiving. How did they hurt us?
4. Forgiveness asks, Are our offenders more than their hurtful, even cruel, behaviors?
5. Forgiveness can give us a feeling of neutrality toward our offenders. But we can go a step further as well.
6. Forgiveness is primarily a gift to ourselves. It's a way to heal and free us from the emotional shackles of the past.
7. Forgiveness can become a daily practice. We can extend forgiveness beyond significant offenses to daily grievances. Daily practice prepares us for forgiving big offenses, as the Amish demonstrated.

Reflection Question

How do you feel about the word "forgiveness?" Do you need to find another word or phrase that would be more comfortable? Perhaps "letting go," "moving on," or "putting the past in the past." Find a word or phrase that works for you.

Practice

Using your notebook:
1. Identify one upsetting or offending situation in which you ordinarily would have gotten angry and stewed on it for days but instead practiced forgiving.
2. What did you tell yourself to let it dissolve?
3. How did that feel?

20

Self-Forgiveness: Releasing Ourselves from Our Past

Letting ourselves be forgiven is one of the most difficult healings we will undertake. And one of the most fruitful.

—Stephen Levine

"Isn't shame a form of having a conscience?" my client, Wendy, wondered aloud. "I mean, if we've done awful stuff, shouldn't we feel ashamed? Isn't that what we deserve?" Wendy was a woman in her fifties who had talked briefly on several occasions about how ashamed she felt about her sexual "promiscuity" as a young adult. She felt she deserved to feel ashamed.

But when I asked if she wanted to understand why she had made those choices, she declined, saying, "I don't want to talk about it. My behavior was awful. I'm so ashamed, and there's a good reason I should feel bad." Then she changed the subject.

Everyone has a list of "awful" behaviors—things they have done or said that they feel ashamed about. To be human is to have this list. Unfortunately, it is also true that people raised in a shaming environment have a longer list. Growing up in a shame-saturated family without support and guidance, feeling broken and worthless, we may make irresponsible choices. Many young adults make irresponsible choices. However, young adults from shame-based families are predisposed to continue making poor choices into adulthood unless they work on healing the false beliefs about themselves and others. Being angry, hurt, confused, or lost without a rudder or a safety net is a perfect recipe for hurtful, unaware, insensitive, and uncaring decisions and behavior. When we feel most ashamed, we most need self-forgiveness.

"As hard as it is to forgive someone else, it's sometimes much harder to forgive ourselves," wrote Doc Childre. (Childre and Martin 1999) But it helps to remember that self-forgiveness is a choice to forgive our *past selves*. These past selves will only heal their shame with our understanding and caring, not our judgment.

Contrary to what you may have thought, self-forgiveness isn't weak or indulgent. It doesn't mean you let yourself off the hook. You remain responsible for what you did, and you must accept that. But through the tools we used earlier to extend forgiveness to others, you can also move out of the deep rut of self-judgment and condemnation and let your past become *your past*.

Early life shame sets us up to make decisions that will set the trajectory of our adult life. Sadly, we could say that shame has teed us up to make poor decisions. For example, when Tangney and Dearing studied shame-prone fifth graders and followed up when the kids were ages eighteen to nineteen, their findings were striking. These kids were likelier than their non-shame-prone peers to have engaged in risky sex-ual activity, used hard drugs and alcohol, been involved with the criminal justice system, made suicide attempts, and been suspended from high school. Shame and negative feelings about ourselves are the breeding ground for doing things that can be painful to face. Understanding is challenging and often complex, but is there a more worthy effort? We have likely longed to have others understand us. How about being the brave person who gives yourself this gift?

The process of self-forgiveness

To extend self-forgiveness, we engage in a *process* simi-lar to the steps we took in forgiving those who hurt and wounded us. Start by listing the things you've done or said that you feel ashamed about. It's important to remember as you make your list that this is not a list to make you feel ashamed. I suggest you start with the incidents that still stick in your mind. Maybe you stole money from your grandmother, or you were taunting and mean to your sib-lings. As a young adult, maybe you had an affair with your best friend's boyfriend. If the list is beginning to feel too painful, stop for a while and work on these misdeeds. Later you can add to your list—when you're ready. The list can be long and very painful. But the purpose of the list isn't to deepen the shame. The objective is to know what you're forgiving yourself for.

Next, we try to understand who we were when we made those regretful choices. Ask yourself, "What was my motiva-tion when I chose those behaviors that hurt others? What was going on with me then?" For example, if you were sexually indiscriminate, were you trying to get love and attention? Everyone needs love and attention. Were you financially overwhelmed and without support when you stole money from your employer? As a mother, were you tired, stressed, and overwhelmed when you lost it and yelled at your kids? Was your wounding from your own childhood unhealed and spewing onto your own children?

We aren't trying to make excuses. The goal is to develop both awareness and a deeper understanding about the choices we made. There's a reason we did these things. There's a reason we hurt others. Self-forgiveness involves looking at our behaviors and going beyond them into the depth of the pain and hurt we were experiencing *at that time*. Rest assured that we're worthy of any efforts we make to understand our past selves.

To begin, identify a specific incident. Then, in your mind's eye, take a few moments to try to see the person you were then. Can you see that part of yourself? If so, ask her, in a kind, friendly way, what was going on with her. Even if you aren't sure about being able to hear your inner selves, listen. It may be an impression, a quick flash of sensing who you were then. Maybe it will feel like a memory. If you sense a feeling of being ashamed, reassure yourself that you aren't judging and simply want to understand what it was like to be your younger self.

When I did this exercise, I was surprised at how often my past-self did things without really considering how others felt; she was primarily concerned about herself. This isn't easy to admit, but I believe it was true. As an adult, I understand she was angry, and her unhealed wounds of rejection propelled some of her careless behavior. As a result, she was often reckless with other people's hearts, maybe because she couldn't feel her own—or theirs. Sadly, she lacked the empathy for others that they deserved. I also understand this is one of the costs of shame—deficient empathy. So, I tried to understand what was happening with my younger self, much like a compassionate mother would. Again, this isn't an excuse. The goal is to develop an understanding that opens the way for compassion.

How about you? As you look at your past self and your insensitive hurtful behaviors, do you see you were confused, overwhelmed, or angry at those times? Did you lack support and guidance? Did you get caught up in addictions? Was belonging to a group of friends more important than doing the right thing? Of course, none of this justifies your behavior, and that's precisely why you're exploring self-forgiveness.

When we don't understand ourselves, we label ourselves as stupid, broken, loser, terrible, disgusting. Or we accept the labels others have tagged on us. When we do that, we reduce ourselves to our behavior, and again, we are not just our behavior. We deserve a more extensive understanding, which can only start with our brave self-exploration. As we face who we were and what we did, we need to find a glimmer of compassion for our younger self. Then we can nurture that compassion by refraining from judging and beating ourselves up. Reviewing, remembering, and becoming aware of our hurtful decisions can be excruciating. However, self-forgiveness allows us—even requires us—to see our worth despite what we've done.

Remember the process of healing our inner parts? As we engage these past selves and try to understand their mindset and circumstances, we are being a kind adult, a compassionate mother or father who loves the errant lost child or young adult no matter the behavior. Not condoning—just understanding and staying open-hearted.

The lasting effects of hurting others

Our next step is both painful and crucial. It asks us to look at our hurtful behavior *and* how it has affected those we hurt. Maybe our grandmother didn't miss the money, and the only one we hurt was ourselves. But sometimes we hurt innocent others. Too often, they are the ones we should have protected but didn't. These choices were not because we were bad but because we were imperfect, wounded, and lacked empathy. Unfortunately, humans make decisions that hurt each other.

As we face how our behavior has affected those we hurt, have courage. Remember that we seek forgiveness *because* we have done or said things that have unfairly hurt others, and it has affected them. If you have mistreated your children, if you mistreated a sister, friend, or sweetheart, accept the responsibility and consequences for your behavior.

This self-examination can feel brutal, so do *not* fall prey to judging yourself. Remember that forgiveness is a gift we extend, including to ourselves, *because* we have unjustly hurt another person. It's a gift because it is *not* something we've earned. We know we've wronged others, and forgiveness is a path that allows us to have mercy and compassion for ourselves regardless of what we've done.

You may not think you deserve forgiveness, and that shame and suffering are what you've earned, but remember research shows shame doesn't make us better people. To judge ourselves as uniquely broken or exceptionally messed up doesn't help anyone. On the contrary, it keeps us stuck and even increases the likelihood of repeating shame-based behavior because our wounds remain unhealed. Shame-based behavior comes from unhealed wounds.

Apologize?

Should you apologize and ask for forgiveness from those you've hurt? This can be a tricky decision. First, ask yourself, what is your motivation? Next, have they shown you any signs that they want an apology?

It's important to be mindful about your motivation. Is it self-serving? For example, apologizing to look good or show them you are morally superior is not a genuine apology. Likewise, it isn't sincere if you *expect* reconciliation or even to try to avoid consequences, such as the damage they can do to your reputation.

If you decide to apologize, the most authentic way of asking for forgiveness is admitting that you hurt them and clearly stating that you sincerely regret the choices you made. The goal, remember, is to apologize and ask for forgiveness for no reason other than because you're sorry about how you hurt them.

Even if your apology is heartfelt, try not to become attached to how the person reacts. You may be disappointed if you have expectations about the person's reaction. Remember that their response will be based on how they feel. If they tell you how much they hate you, accept that they hate you. They have the right to their own process. When or if they ever forgive you is up to them.

On the other hand, an apology given and received, and forgiveness offered and accepted, are powerful healing opportunities for all. There is something profound that happens when you use the words, "Please forgive me."

A friend who I'll call Catherine talked with me after her son, now twenty-eight, told her he had been sexually abused at a boarding school he attended as a pre-teen. She was devastated and blamed herself. When her son was young, she had an alcohol addiction, and when she finally divorced, her addiction worsened as her ex-husband and his new wife bullied, threatened, and shamed her repeatedly. Then, Catherine was diagnosed with stage four breast cancer and sought specialized treatment at a facility far from the home she shared with her son. She had to relocate for several months for daily treatment, and her son's father refused to allow her son to be with her. When she moved, she left her son in the care of his father. Later she learned her son felt she abandoned him.

When she returned home, her son chose to remain primarily with his father and stepmother. A year later, his attitude and mediocre grades became too much for his father. With the support of a therapist, the father and stepmother decided to send the boy to a boarding school. "I knew he was too young to be sent away," Catherine told me.

"When his grades didn't improve, I felt there was more to his grades than simply not doing his homework. Something else was going on with him. I knew something was wrong in that boarding school. But I couldn't hold my own against his father, stepmother, and therapist. They all thought it was the perfect place and a good decision. I feel so much shame." She paused and said, "I was terrified of my ex and his new wife. I couldn't and didn't know how to cope, so I drank a lot. I was a drunk. I wasn't there for my son like I should have been. I should never have allowed him to go to the boarding school. I should have done more. I have so much shame."

"What did you say to your son when he told you about his abuse at the school?" I asked Catherine.

"I told him I was so sorry," she said. "I told him, 'I'm so sorry I wasn't there for you like I should have been. I'm so sorry. I can see how hurt you are. I'm so grateful you shared this with me now.'" She said that they both cried, and she listened until he finished talking. "It didn't seem like much else needed to be said right then. He said he felt better, we agreed to talk again, and we made dinner."

"But I still feel so much shame," Catherine continued, "and I knew after that conversation, my son hadn't forgiven me. When we talked again, he told me in order to fully forgive me, he needed me to acknowledge that I had abandoned him when I went for cancer treatment and then again at the boarding school. He wanted no excuses like that I had to go away for treatment. He needed me to say, 'I'm sorry I abandoned you.' Saying I was sorry wasn't enough. He needed me to acknowledge his need to hear that I had abandoned him. This was so hard to say. In my mind and heart, I hadn't abandoned him, yet that's how he felt. But it wasn't about me—it was about healing for both of us."

Catherine hoped having her son forgive her would bring the healing and peace they both desired. But there was another layer that was not yet within her awareness. She needed to work on self-forgiveness. Her son couldn't provide that. She had to do that work herself.

Finding self-compassion

How did Catherine ease her shame? How was she able to move toward self-compassion? As Catherine shared with another friend her feelings of shame and self-condemnation, her friend asked, "You have such compassion for others. So why not for yourself?" Catherine replied, "That's a good question." She needed to look at who she was when she could not be there for her son and offer forgiveness to that self. These negative judgments about herself as her son's mother were eating her up. Catherine understood she was overusing alcohol to try to numb the pain of her own abusive childhood, abusive marriage, and divorce. While it was not pleasant to reflect on those times, it was necessary to under-stand the self she was then. As Pema Chodron said, "Having compassion starts and ends with having compassion for all those unwanted parts of ourselves, all those imperfections that we don't even want to look at. Compassion isn't some kind of self-improvement project or ideal that we're trying to live up too." (Chodron 2016)

As Catherine was able to step back from her blinding shame, she saw that in her heart, she wanted only the best for her beloved son. She didn't want to be his drunk mother. But she was unable to change direction at that time, and her boy suffered terribly. Of course, there are no excuses, but again, we aren't looking for excuses. We're looking for self-understanding, self-compassion, and self-forgiveness.

Catherine couldn't be emotionally available to her son when he needed her as a boy, but he still needs her now. She could give him something now that she couldn't provide until she stopped being afraid to look at herself and understand the fear and shame that created her decision to drink. By engaging in the self-forgiveness process, she is now able to be emotionally connected to his deep hurt without making excuses, minimizing her role, or feeling sorry for herself.

Never underestimate the healing of a sincere apology. Your willingness to let the ones you have offended tell you how you've hurt them is part of apologizing too. They may need something from you, not just an apology but an acknowledgment of what it was like for them. Catherine was able to provide that for her son. Remaining lost in shame benefits no one. As her son continued to tell her about some of his experiences, even though it was painful to hear, she listened until each time he wanted to talk about it.

Stop beating yourself up

Tara Brach (2011) asked the question, "Why do we hold on tightly to our belief in our deficiency? Why are we so loyal to our suffering, so addicted to our self-judgment?" As we saw in a previous chapter, self-compassion is a monumental task for all shame-prone folks. When we see ourselves as flawed and defective, self-compassion may seem like a cop-out. We may feel totally undeserving. However, our self-judgment and the judgment we have received from others—can be overcome. First, we must consciously decide to stop beating ourselves up. Let's remember that a beat-up self is not good for anyone.

Berating yourself, talking about your shameful behavior, and even continuing to talk about how sorry you are when the other person has gotten the message only serves to do the very thing you don't want to do—interfere with the emotional connection you can offer to those in your life now. In Catherine's case, her son wants an engaged, emotionally available mother who can acknowledge how he felt abandoned by her, not a mother making excuses, beaten down by her own shame and fear. She needed to work on self-forgiveness to give this to her son.

Too often, when we feel ashamed of our behavior, we unconsciously believe that we deserve to be punished. And sometimes, we try to assuage our shame without forgiving ourselves. We do other things to make amends without directly addressing our need to forgive ourselves.

Here's an example: As a young adult, one client I knew was involved with a gang that sold and trafficked copious amounts of methamphetamines. Later, as a dentist, she felt so guilty about her involvement in fostering addiction that she thought she didn't deserve to make the money her profession afforded her. She also knew that meth was deadly for users' teeth. So, she undercharged for her dental services, she didn't pursue money owed to her, and gave large sums to friends and even strangers. She felt terrible and ashamed of the havoc and addictions she had fostered. This was her way of making reparations, she said. But as well-meaning as she might have been, the gift she needed to give was to herself—the gift of self-forgiveness. I encouraged her to explore self-compassion and self-forgiveness as part of her healing process. Deciding to contribute to others from a place of self-forgiveness is much better for everyone than giving to others out of shame.

We all must decide if we will let the shame-filled behavior of our past selves be forgiven. Even if we believe we don't deserve it, we can choose to begin the journey. No matter how egregious our behavior was, we can finally heal our shame and free ourselves from shame's tyranny. It's a gift of mercy to ourselves. Without it, we're stuck in a past that we can't change, and we're emotionally unavailable to love and support others who are in our lives. When we remain stuck in self-loathing and self-blame, we're unhappy and preoccupied with our inner turmoil. Does that serve anyone? No, it doesn't.

———

Chapter Takeaways

1. Self-forgiveness is much needed, but something we often don't give to ourselves. Many times we don't believe we deserve it. It is an essential step in healing from past mistakes.

2. Understanding the motivations and circumstances that led to our hurtful actions allows us to gain insight into our past selves and develop empathy toward them. This is not about taking ourselves off the hook but recognizing that our behavior often stems from unresolved wounds.

3. Apologizing and seeking forgiveness can be a significant step in the healing process. However, our apologies must be genuine and motivated by a sincere desire to make amends. It's not about seeking validation or reconciliation.

4. Continuously beating ourselves up over past mistakes only perpetuates shame and interferes with us being emotionally unavailable for others.

Embracing self-forgiveness benefits us *and* those who need us to be emotionally present in their lives today.

Reflection question

If you forgave yourself for one of your big past mistakes, what kind of energy and mind space would that open for you?

Practice

Have your notebook ready to go.

1. What past mistakes do you still regret and feel bad about? Did this chapter help you decide to begin the process of forgiving yourself?
2. Set aside some time to enter into a self-forgiveness conversation with yourself. No matter what mistakes you may have made and how the offended person has reacted, the ultimate forgiveness must come from you.
3. Be sure to remember who you were at the time of the offense and the circumstances that led to your behavior. This may be difficult to face. Refer to chapters 9 and 10 for a review of how to approach yourself.
4. Remember always to speak to your self parts as you would speak to a friend.

21

Finding Meaning in Our Suffering

*No one can ever do anything more worthy of self-respect than
to break the grip of a painful past she never deserved and walk
dangerously with hope into the possibility of tomorrow.*

Lewis Smedes

Some believe that everything happens for a reason and
while we may not know if this is true, I do know we can
use whatever happens to us for a good purpose. I'm author-
ing this book to help others who have suffered a life of never
feeling good enough. I wanted to provide insights and tools
to make their journey shorter and less painful.

When our pain is great, we have a purpose—healing
ourselves. Sometimes, our purpose is to "show those bas-
tards they didn't get the best of me." Sometimes, we just so
desperately want to feel better. But facing our wounding and
the pain we endured can be so difficult at times that we can
lose hope. Everyone needs at least a glimmer of hope that
their lives have worth and that someone—a faithful dog or
cuddling cat—needs them. Your friends, co-workers, members of your support groups, your neighbors, and people you

have yet to meet need your example that evil doesn't win. I have cheered in my heart many times when clients could see that their despair didn't need to triumph.

A purpose in serving others

The incest survivors in Enright's forgiveness study found a purpose they hadn't anticipated. "After participants experienced emotional relief from the traumas, a number of them expressed an intent to become counselors for other incest survivors."

In a similar vein, members of AA routinely volunteer to sponsor new members. One of the powers of AA is the relationship between the sponsor (one who has been sober for a length of time and uses the principles of AA in their life) and those who need support and guidance to stay sober. The sponsors, who know what it means to cover their pain with substances, find purpose in helping others who are trying to reclaim their lives—both sponsor and sponsee benefit.

When anyone can break the cycles of abuse that have haunted their families for generations, they can feel very proud because the abuse stopped with them. Stopping domestic violence, drug abuse, and using shame on our children or anyone—is a beautiful gift. For many who have done this, it is one of their proudest accomplishments and certainly worthy of our deep gratitude.

"Every problem suggests a question: are you ready to embody what you say you believe? Can you reach within yourself for enough clarity, strength, forgiveness, serenity, love, patience, and faith to turn this around? That is the spiritual meaning of every situation: not what happened to us, but what we do with what happened to us. The next step is deciding who we want to become because of what happened to us. The only real failure is the failure to grow from what we went through." (Williamson 2004)

Your purpose can be your North Star as you plot out what you will do with the life you have reclaimed from shame. You may not know what purpose you have. You may incorrectly think that purpose is some grand calling, but your purpose can be your example of your tenacious efforts to heal and forgive. You have no idea how your lived example inspires others who may have little or no hope. That's a priceless gift and one that is unique to you.

To make something good come from bad often takes fierce determination. Here are some true stories from clients (names changed) that illustrate their pathway to a positive purpose.

When my client, Susanna, was about eight, she told her mother that her uncle had sexually abused her. Her mother refused to talk with her for weeks. And it wasn't just her uncle's abuse. Her entire childhood was full of abuse and betrayal. But she had a gift. From an early age, she had a strong, beautiful voice, and she would sing in the cotton fields of her parents' east Oklahoma farm.

When she finally left home, she began singing in bars and clubs. Her voice and life experience resonated with the highs and lows of the blues and the straightforward feelings of country western songs. Her voice was powerful and stirring, touching the listeners who needed to hear the tones and lyrics of suffering and redemption. For Susanna and her audiences, these songs were inspirational.

Kim is a woman who uses her suffering to understand and help others. As a psychiatrist, she works with the mentally ill homeless. Her own struggle with drugs, homelessness, abuse, and neglect makes her the perfect doctor to listen to her struggling patients. She knows their pain and hopelessness. As a physician, she can offer medication, empathy, and respect. Her amazing journey to medical school and her psychiatry residency demonstrate each day that the cruelty and injustices she suffered didn't triumph. Service to this challenging and underserved community helps her find meaning and purpose in her own complicated life. This is the legacy she is creating.

The Amish community knows the importance of extending forgiveness as a daily practice. When the tragedy befell their community, they weren't merely resuscitating an old moral belief. Forgiveness was an active way of life for them. We can practice forgiveness every day as well. We have endless opportunities. Consider how you react when someone cuts you off in traffic. Are your kids in the car? Your friend or spouse? What are you modeling for them? How do you react when you're stood up by a friend who agreed to meet you for coffee? So many everyday experiences beg for forgiveness instead of resentment.

Some of us come from families where one family member doesn't speak to another because of something that happened years ago. While it's okay to decide who we want to affiliate with, family members who carry grudges model for the children and other relatives, that it is what the family does. How much better would it be for you to model and teach about forgiveness? This does not mean that we have to then reconcile and invite them for dinner. Sometimes that is not safe or appropriate. But forgiving helps to lift the burden of resentment. Then we can decide what we want to do, if anything.

In a culture that entertains viewers with revenge stories, will you be a champion for forgiveness? Will you teach your children to forgive? Will you speak up when your friends or family talk about getting even? Will you engage those who are in the habit of holding on to resentments in a conversation about forgiveness?

Your legacy of healing

Your sweetheart, children, grandchildren, neighbors, siblings, and colleagues will remember you by your example. Would you want to be remembered as someone who kept to themselves because they felt broken and worthless? Or someone whose anger and resentment spilled into their family life and parenting? Of course not, and you have a choice. You don't have to be free of all your childhood demons to change your behavior toward others.

Do you want to be remembered as a mother owning up to her mistakes and moving on or a woman so wracked with the pain of her past mistakes that she's sullen, depressed, ashamed, and self-sacrificing? Would you prefer being recognized as someone who felt appropriate remorse for their hurtful behavior, changed their ways, apologized sincerely, forgave themselves, and moved on? Through forgiveness, all boats are lifted, and the peace we all long for washes over us like sunlight bathing the hills at sunrise.

If you want to be present, emotionally available, loving, and accepting of those who need you now, you must heal your past. Give this to yourself, consciously work at it, and all who know you will be touched by your presence and grateful. That means healing your shame and forgiving yourself.

Will you choose to be of service? According to research from Emory University, when you are kind to another person, your brain's pleasure and reward centers light up, as if *you* were the recipient of the good deed—not the giver. This phenomenon is called the "helper's high."

In another study called the Rabbit Effect, Kelli Harding, a physician specializing in the study of acts of kindness, wrote, "In 1978, researchers looking at the connection between high cholesterol and heart health in rabbits made a startling discovery. Feeding the rabbits the same high-fat diet, the scientists expected that all would have similar clogging of their arteries. Yet one group had 60 percent fewer fatty deposits than the other. Eventually, they identified the variable: the group that had significantly better health outcomes was under the care of an unusually affectionate researcher who talked to them, cuddled, and petted them, while the other group was simply fed. In other words, the one researcher was kind." Dr. Harding continued, "The rabbit study was just the beginning of what we now know from decades of public health research—our social world is the major predictor of our health. As a medical doctor, I was shocked to learn medical care, while critical, only accounts for about 10–20% of our overall health status. Instead, much of good health depends on creating supportive relationships in our homes, neighborhoods, schools, workplaces, and communities. This means every person's kind or unkind choices in their daily lives makes a difference in the health of others." (Columbia University Department of Psychiatry 2023)

Use your suffering for good. Don't let all that you have been through go to waste. Decide how you will let it shape you and be one of those people who is remembered for their legacy of healing, forgiveness, service, and love. "When people practice forgiveness long enough, they see that they have a choice in life of the legacy they will leave the world. They can leave a legacy of woundedness and anger or a legacy of love and forgiveness." (Enright 2001)

Your suffering wasn't for nothing. You have gifts to give, and we all need your contributions. We all benefit from the work you do to love and appreciate yourself. And thank you for forgiving yourself and others that the light you bring into this world can be seen and be an inspiration to others.

Chapter Takeaways

1. Our suffering can be a catalyst for personal growth and transformation. We can use our painful experiences to find a greater purpose in life, whether it's helping others, advocating for change, or becoming a more compassionate person.
2. We can choose to leave a legacy of love, forgiveness, and healing, even in the face of past pain and suffering.

Reflection Question

Will your legacy differ from the legacy your family may have left you?

Practice

Have your notebook handy.

1. What gifts and strengths do you have that could benefit and encourage others?
2. What specific activities have you been drawn to where you can use your gifts and talents? Perhaps writing a book, volunteering at a charity, forming a book group that reads empowering authors, becoming a therapist, painting art that uplifts and inspires, becoming a Big Sister or Big brother, taking meals to neighbors who need a little love, working at an animal shelter, there are so many opportunities.
3. Have you noticed yourself being more compassionate to others as you have worked on healing your past? Consider this a meaningful contribution and perhaps the purpose of all our lives. Extending compassion to others is a priceless gift.

I hope reading this book has been helpful to you. Remember that healing the wounds of a troubled childhood can be difficult and painful. Reread the chapters that applied to you the most and do the exercises. Reach out for support and seek professional help if you feel lost, defeated, or hopeless. Remember, even as I focused on the core wounding of shame and did lots of parts work, my healing took years. Don't give up on your healing. Although it is not guaranteed, it is possible. We need your presence and your example of healing, which is always a work in progress. As Peter Levine teaches, anyone suffering from trauma has a valuable story to tell, and when we share our stories of healing, we hold out a light to others that there is hope, dignity and a path to wholeness. This is how we end the epidemic of shame and free ourselves to be the person we were born to be

Acknowledgments

As I reflect on the many individuals who have guided and inspired me throughout my personal and professional journey, I am deeply grateful for the countless gifts you have shared with me. To those I can name and to those who must remain nameless—my clients—you have all been cherished companions along the way. My world is immeasurably richer because of your presence, and I hope you know how much I value and honor your contributions

I sincerely appreciate my colleagues who have listened and generously shared their clinical wisdom with me over the decades. I am particularly grateful to the consulting group of the "I Street" therapists.

Thank you to those who directly helped me write and edit this book:

To Corinne Lillie, who encouraged me to keep going and helped me heal the wounds I discovered in myself as I wrote. Your presence in my life is one of my life's greatest gifts.

Immense gratitude to Sierra Hampton-Eng, who read a very rough draft and still encouraged me. Your friendship, suggestions, and perspective mean so much to me.

I am grateful to my editor, Sara Kendrick, for her spot-on suggestions and encouragement and to Jill Ronsley and Glen Edelstein for their amazing design contributions.

And to my life partner of forty years, Leslie, who patiently read every word many times and offered her professional advice and endless encouragement.

To all the authors and talented clinicians whose work I draw on throughout this book, I am especially grateful to Patricia De Young, Janina Fisher, Bessel van der Kolk, Rhonda Dearing, June Price, and Robert Enright.

Resources

Compassion

Earley, J. *Self-therapy: A Step-by-Step Guide to Creating Wholeness and Healing Your Inner Child Using IFS, a New Cutting-edge Psychotherapy*. Larkspur, CA: Patterns System Books. 2009.

Earley website

Self-compassion

Paul Gilbert, http://www.mindfulcompassion.com

Kristin Neff, https://self-compassion.org

Check out the self-compassion assessment.

Heart Healing and Guidance

Childre, D and Howard Martin. *The HeartMath Solution*. New York: Harper One. 1999.

Childre, Martin. *Heart Intelligence: Connecting with the Intuitive Guidance of the Heart*. Ada, Michigan: Waterfront Press. 2016.

Website: https://www.heartmath.org

Empathy deficient disorder

Stout, Martha. *The Sociopath Next Door*. New York: Broadway Books. 2005.

Orloff, Judith. *The Genius of Empathy*. Boulder: Sounds True. 2024.

Recommended Book about Trauma and Healing

Van der Kolk, B. *The Body Keeps Score: Brain, Mind, and Body in the Healing of Trauma*. New York: Penguin Press. 2014.

Fisher, J. *Healing the Fragmented Selves of Trauma Survivors: Overcoming self-Alienation*. New York: Routledge. 2017.

Inner Child and Internal Family Systems

Schwartz, Richard. *Introduction to the Internal Family Systems Model*. Oak Park, Illinois: Trailheads Publishing. 2001.

Relationships

Gottman, J and Silver, N. *The Seven Principles for Making Marriages Work*. New York, Harmony Press. 2015.

Gottman Institute: https://gottman.com

Johnson, Sue. *Hold Me Tight: Seven Conversations for a Lifetime of Love*. New York: Little brown Spark. 2008.

Engel, Beverly. *Escaping Emotional Abuse: Healing from the Shame You Don't Deserve*. New York: Citadel. 2020.

Meditation

Zinn, Jon Kabot and Thich Nat Hanh. *Full Catastrophe Living: Using the Wisdom of Your Body and Mind to Face Stress, Pain, Illness*. New York: Random House. 2009.

Kornfield, Jack. *A Path with Heart: A Guide Through the Perils and Promises of a Spiritual Life*. New York: Random House. 2009.

Forgiveness

Enright, R. *Forgiveness Is a Choice*. Washington, DC: American Psychological Association. 2001.

Enright, R. and Fitzgibbons, R. *Forgiveness Therapy: An Empirical Guide for Resolving Anger and Restoring Hope*. Washington, DC: American Psychological Association. 2015.

International Forgiveness Institute. https://internationalforgiveness.com (Check out their free self-assessments.)

Smedes, Lewis. *The Art of Forgiving: When You Need to Forgive and Don't Know How*. New York: Random House. 1996.

Bibliography

Allison, Ralph, and Ted Schwarz. 1999. *Minds in Many Pieces: Revealing the Spiritual Side of Multiple Personality Disorder.* Vienna: Cie Pub.

Bennet, E.A. 1983. *What Jung Really Said.* New York: Schocken Books.

Brach, Tara. 2011. https://www.tarabrach.com/. July 1. https://www.tarabrach.com/inquiring-trance/.

—. n.d. Tara Brach. https://www.tarabrach.com/guided-meditations/.

Bradshaw, John. 1988. *Healing the Shame That Binds You.* Deerfield: Health Communications, Inc.

Brown, Brene. 2007. *I Thought It Was Just Me (but It Isn't).* New York: Penguin Random House LLC.

—. 2010. *The Gifts of Imperfection: Let Go of Who You Think You're Supposed to Be and Embrace Who You Are.* Center City: Hazelden Publishing.

Brown, J. Wong, J. 2017. "How gratitude changes you and your brain." *Greater Good Magazine.* June 6. https://greatergood.berkeley.edu/article/item/how_gratitude_changes_you_and_your_brain.

Childre, D, and D Rozman. 2005. *Transforming Stress: The HeartMath Solution for Relieving Worry, Fatigue, and Tension.* Oakland: New Harbinger.

Childre, Doc, and Howard Martin. 1999. *The HeartMath Solution.* New York: Harper Collins Publisher.

Chodron, Pema. 2016. *When Things Fall Apart: Heart Advise for Difficult Times.* Boulder: Shambhala.

Cuddy, Emily, and Richard Reeves. 2014. *Hitting Kids: American Parenting and Physical Punishment.* November 6. www.brookings.edu/research/hitting-kids-american-parenting-and-physical-punishment/.

Dearing, Rhonda, and June Price Tangney. 2011. *Shame in the Therapy Hour.* Washington D.C.: American Psychological Association.

Decety, Jean. 2010. "The Neurodevelopment of Empathy in Humans." *Developmental Neuroscience.* 257-263.

DeYoung, Patricia. 2015. *Understanding and Treating Chronic Shame.* New York: Routledge.

Earley, Jay. 2009. *Self-Therapy: A Step By Step Guide to Creating Wholeness and Healing Your Inner Child Using IFT, a New, Cutting-Edge Psychotherapy.* Larkspur: Pattern System Books.

Earley, John. n.d. "How it works." *Self-Therapy Journey.* selftherapyjourney.com/Pattern/Beginning/How_STJ_Works.aspx.

Eisenberg-Berg, N, and C Neal. 1979. "Children's moral reasoning on their own spontaneous prosocial behavior." https://psycnet.apa.org/record/1979-28166-001.

Emmons, Robert. 2010. *Why Gratitude is Good.* November 16. https://greatergood.berkeley.edu/article/item/why_gratitude_is_good/.

Engel, Beverly. 2020. *Escaping Emotional Abuse: Healing from the Shame You Don't Deserve.* New York: Citadel.

—. 2006. *Healing Your Emotional Self: A Powerful Program to Help You Raise Your Self-Esteem, Quiet Your Inner Critic, and Overcome Your Shame.* New York: John Wiley.

Enright, Robert. 2015. *8 Keys to Forgiveness.* New York: W. W. Norton and Company.

—. 2001. *Forgiveness Is a Choice: A Step-by-Step Process for Resolving Anger and Restoring Hope.* Washington D.C.: American Psychological Association.

—. n.d. International Forgiveness Institute. https://internationalforgiveness.com/.

—. 2012. *The Forgiving Life.* Washington D.C.: American Psychological Association.

Enright, Robert, and R Fitzgibbons. 2015. *Forgiveness therapy.* Washington D.C.: American Psychological Association.

Finke, Leigh. 2015. *Yes! Solutions Journalism.* Oct 14. https://www.yesmagazine.org/health-happiness/2015/10/14/researchers-say-watching-movies-helps-you-work-your-empathy-muscle.

Fisher, Janina. 2017. *Healing the Fragmented Selves of Trauma Survivors: Overcoming Self-Alienation.* New York: Routledge.

Gandhi, Mahatma. 1995. *All Men Are Brothers: Life and Thoughts of Mahatma Gandhi, As Told in His Own Words.* Ahmedabad: Navajivan.

Gibson, Lindsey. 2015. *Adult Children of Emotionally Immature Parents: How to Heal from Distant, Rejecting, or Self-Involved Parents.* Oakland: New Harbinger.

Gilbert, Paul. 2022. *Compassion Focused Therapy.* Oxfordshire: Routledge.

Goleman, D. 1997. *Healing Emotions: Conversations with the Dalai Lama on Mindfulness, Emotions, and Health.* Boston: Shambhala Publications.

Gottman, John and Nan Silver. 2015. *The Seven Principles for Making Marriage Work: A Practical Guide from the Country's Foremost Relationship Expert.* New York: Harmony.

Hanh, T. N. 2010. *Reconciliation: Healing the Inner Child.* Berkeley: Parallax Press.

Herman, J. "Shattered shame states and their repair." In Judy Yellin and Kate White, editors. 2012. *Shattered States: Disorganized Attachment & its Repair.* New York: Routledge.

Holmes, T. 2016. "Spirituality in systemic practice: an internal family systems perspective." Accessed April 4, 2018. wingedheart.org.

Johnson, Sue. 2008. *Hold Me Tight: Seven Conversations for a Lifetime of Love.* New York: Little Brown Spark.

—. 2019. *The Practice of Emotionally Focused Couple Therapy: Creating Connection.* New York: Routledge.

Kaufman, G. 1989. *The Psychology of Shame: Theory and Treatment of Shame-Based Syndromes.* New York: Springer Publishing.

Kelley, V. Jr., and M. Lamia. 2018. *The Upside of Shame: Therapeutic Interventions Using the Positive Aspects of a "Negative" Emotion.* New York: Norton.

Kornfield, Jack. 2008. *The Wise Heart: Buddhist Psychology for the West.* London: Ebury Publishing.

Kraybill, Donald, Steve Nolt, and David Weaver-Zercher. 2010. *Amish Grace: How Forgiveness Transcended Tragedy.* San Francisco: Jossey-Bass.

Levine, Peter. 2015. *Traumatic Memory: Brain and Body in a Search for the Living Past*. Berkeley: North Atlantis Books.

Lewis, Helen. 1971. "Shame and guilt in neurosis." *Psychoanalytic Review* 419-438.

Li, Qing. 2018. *Forest Bathing: How Trees Can Help Us Find Health and Happiness*. New York: Viking Press.

Marsh, Jason. 2011. *Tips for Keeping a Gratitude Journal*. November 17. https://greatergood.berkeley.edu/article/item/tips_for_keeping_a_gratitude_journal.

Maté, Gabor and Daniel Mate. 2022. *The Myth of Normal: Trauma, Illness, and Healing in a Toxic Culture*. New York: Avery Publishing.

Mathew McKay, Jeffery Wood, Jeffery Brantly. 2019. *The Dialectical Behavioral Therapy Skills Workbook*. Oakland: New Harbinger.

McCarty, Rollin. 2001. *Science of the Heart*. Boulder Creek: HeartMath Research Center.

Miller, Alice. 1990. *For Your Own Good: Hidden Cruelty in Child-Rearing and the Roots of Violence*. New York: Farrar Straus Giroux.

Nathanson, N.T. 1992. *Shame and Pride: Affect, Sex, and the Birth of the Self*. New York: W. W. Norton and Company.

Neff, Kristin. 2015. *Self-Compassion: The Proven Power of Being Kind to Yourself*. New York: William Morrow Paperbacks.

Neff, Kristin, Kristin Kirkpatric, and Stephanie Rude. 2007. "Self-compassion and adaptive psychological functioning." *Journal of Research in Personality* 139-154.

Porges, Stephen. 2011. *The Polyvagal Theory: Neurophysiological Foundation of Emotions, Attachment, Communication, and Self-Regulation.* New York: W. W. Norton and Company.

Schore, A. N. 2015. *The Science and Art of Psychotherapy.* New York: W. W. Norton & Company.

Schwartz, Richard. 2021. *No Bad Parts: Healing Trauma and Restoring Wholeness with Internal Family Systems Model.* Louisville: Sounds True.

Siegel, Daniel. 2021. *Becoming Aware: A 21-Day Mindfulness Program for Reducing Anxiety and Cultivating Calm.* Los Angeles: TarcherPerigee.

Smedes, Lewis. 1993. *Shame and Grace.* New York: Harper Collins.

—. 1997. *The Art of Forgiving: When You Need to Forgive and Don't Know How.* New York: Random House.

Spock, Benjamin. 1946. *The Common Sense Book of Baby and Child Care.* New York City: Gallery Books.

Stout, Martha. 2005. *The Sociopath Next Door.* New York: Broadway Books.

Tangney, Jane, and Rhonda Dearing. 2002. *Shame and Guilt.* New York: Guilford Press.

The School of Life. 2019. *How to Overcome Your Childhood.* London: The School of Life.

Thomas, Katherine Woodward. 2004, 2021. *Calling in the One: Seven Weeks to Attract the Love of Your Life.* New York: Harmony Books.

Tronick. https://www.youtube.com/watch?v=f1Jw0-LExyc

Trump, Mary. 2020. *Too Much and Never Enough: How My Family Created the World's Most Dangerous Man.* New York: Simon and Shuster.

Tutu, Desmond, and Mpho Tutu. 2015. *The Book of Forgiving: The Fourfold Path for Healing Ourselves and Our World.* New York: HarperOne.

Van der Kolk, Bassel. 2014. *The Body Keeps Score: Brain, Mind and Body in the Healing of Trauma.* New York: Penguin Random House.

Villamil, Andrew, Talya Vogel, Elli Weisbaum, and Daniel J Siegel. 2019. "Cultivating Well-Being through the Three Pillars of Mind Training: Understanding How Training the Mind Improves Physiological and Psychological Well-Being."

Walters, Joanna. 2016. "The happening": 10 years after the Amish shooting." *The Guardian,* October 2.

Watson, John B. 1928. *Psychological Care of Infant and Child.* New York: W. W. Norton and Company.

Webb, Jonice and Christine Musello. 2012. *Running on Empty: Overcoming Your Childhood Emotional Neglect.* New York: Morgan James Publishing.

Wilber, Ken. 2000. *Integral Psychology.* Boston: Shambhala Press.

Williamson, Marianne. 2004. "The gift of change: spiritual guidance for living your best life." In *The Gift of Change: Spiritual Guidance for Living Your Best Life,* by Marianne Williamson. New York: HarperOne.

Wilson, Sandra. 1992. *Shame-Free Parenting.* Downers Grove: Intervarsity Press.

Woods, Hanna, and Michael Proeve. 2014. "Relationship of mindfulness, self-compassion and meditation experiences with shame-proneness." *Journal of Cognitive Psychotherapy,* 20-33.

Yarnell, Lisa, Kristin Neff, Oliver Davidson, and Michael Mullarkey. n.d. *Running on Empty: Overcome Your Childhood Emotional Neglect*

Yirka, Bob. 2023. MedicalExpress.com. January 6. https://medicalxpress.com/news/2023-01-cyclic-technique-effective-stress-mindfulness.html.

Index

A

P

Parenting
  advice, history of 91
  shame versus guilt practices 96, 100
Parts
  as ingenious survivors 108
  attachment bond with 181
  collection of 107
  communication from 110, 121
  healing process 135
  hijacked by 124
  making contact with 126
    as with a friend 128
    examples of 130
    purpose of encounters 136
  protectors, role of 137
  subpersonalities 106, 111
  that carry shame-speak beliefs 148
Perfection 48, 152
Porges, Stephen 31
Projection
  definition of 47
  examples of 189, 191

R

Relationships
  harsh start up 221
  identifying our patterns 217
  identifying what we want 223
  potential, mistaken belief of 226
Repetition compulsion
  definition of 214
Revenge, seeking 154, 248
Rhesus monkey
  experiment 37
Rumi 119

S

School of Life 41, 159
Schore, Allan 24, 40
Schreber, Moritz 91
Schwartz, Richard 113, 122, 134, 140

W